MEMORABLE MOMENTS IN ONE-DAY CRICKET

Andy Capostagno

PENGUIN BOOKS

PENGUIN BOOKS

Published by the Penguin Group
80 Strand, London WC2R 0RL, England
Penguin Putnam Inc, 375 Hudson Street, New York,
New York 10014, USA
Penguin Books Australia Ltd, 250 Camberwell Road, Camberwell,
Victoria 3124, Australia
Penguin Books Canada Ltd, 10 Alcorn Avenue, Toronto,
Ontario, Canada M4V 3B2
Penguin Books (NZ) Ltd, Cnr Rosedale and Airborne Roads, Albany,
Auckland, New Zealand
Penguin Books India (P) Ltd, 11 Community Centre, Panchsheel Park,
New Delhi – 110 017, India
Penguin Books (South Africa) (Pty) Ltd, 24 Sturdee Avenue, Rosebank,
Johannesburg 2196, South Africa

Penguin Books (South Africa) (Pty) Ltd, Registered Offices:
Second Floor, 90 Rivonia Road, Sandton 2196, South Africa

First published by Penguin Books (South Africa) (Pty) Ltd 2002

Copyright © Text: Andy Capostagno 2002
Copyright © Photographs: As per individual credits
Copyright © Cover images: Duif du Toit/Touchline Photo, Getty Images/Touchline Photo
All rights reserved
The moral right of the author has been asserted

ISBN 0143 02411 6

Typesetting and design: Mouse Design
Printed and bound by Formeset Printers, Cape Town

Except in the United States of America, this book is sold subject to the condition that it shall not, by way of trade or otherwise, be lent, resold, hired out, or otherwise circulated without the publisher's prior consent in any form of binding or cover other than that in which it is published and without a similar condition including this condition being imposed on the subsequent purchaser.

Contents

Acknowledgements	v
Introduction	1
The Birth of One-Day International Cricket	5
The First World Cup	13
England	27
West Indies	43
India	57
Australia	71
South Africa	81
Pakistan	103
Sri Lanka	117
Kenya	129
New Zealand	135
Bangladesh	143
Zimbabwe	151
Epilogue	163

Acknowledgements

This book is not in chronological order, nor is it in the order by which sides were granted Test status, or any other order for that matter. If it makes it to a second edition I might change the order. However, it would not have been possible without help of the highest order. Ian Mills of Touchline Photo found pictures that I thought did not exist, thereby enriching the text beyond what it probably deserves.

The Cricinfo website was an inexhaustible source of facts and the editor of its South African branch, Peter Robinson, was kind enough to run his professional glass eye over my copy. The Capostagno Trust provided me with a tranquil environment in which to write, Rodney Hartman found a missing scorecard and Wain Stanton gave me the benefit of his leaky memory.

Many great cricketers gave me their time and thoughts, among them my boyhood hero, Barry Richards, of whom I was so in awe that I forgot to press the 'record' button. Michael Holding, Ravi Shastri, Jonty Rhodes, Ken Rutherford, Stephen Jack, Garth le Roux, Andrew Hall, Roger Prideaux, Mike Haysman, Adrian Kuiper, Hylton Ackerman, Robin Jackman and Trevor Quirk all helped me to a greater or lesser extent. Thanks to you all.

But there was one cricketer who gave more than most to this book and will not get to see the results. He fell from grace in the cricket world, but never lost his own personal grace. From my office window I can see the mountain into which the plane that was carrying him home to his wife Bertha crashed in the early morning of Saturday 1 June 2002. In the last year of his life I was fortunate enough to get to know him as more than just a face at a press conference. Hansie Cronjé was my friend. This book is dedicated to him.

Andy Capostagno
Fancourt
June 2002

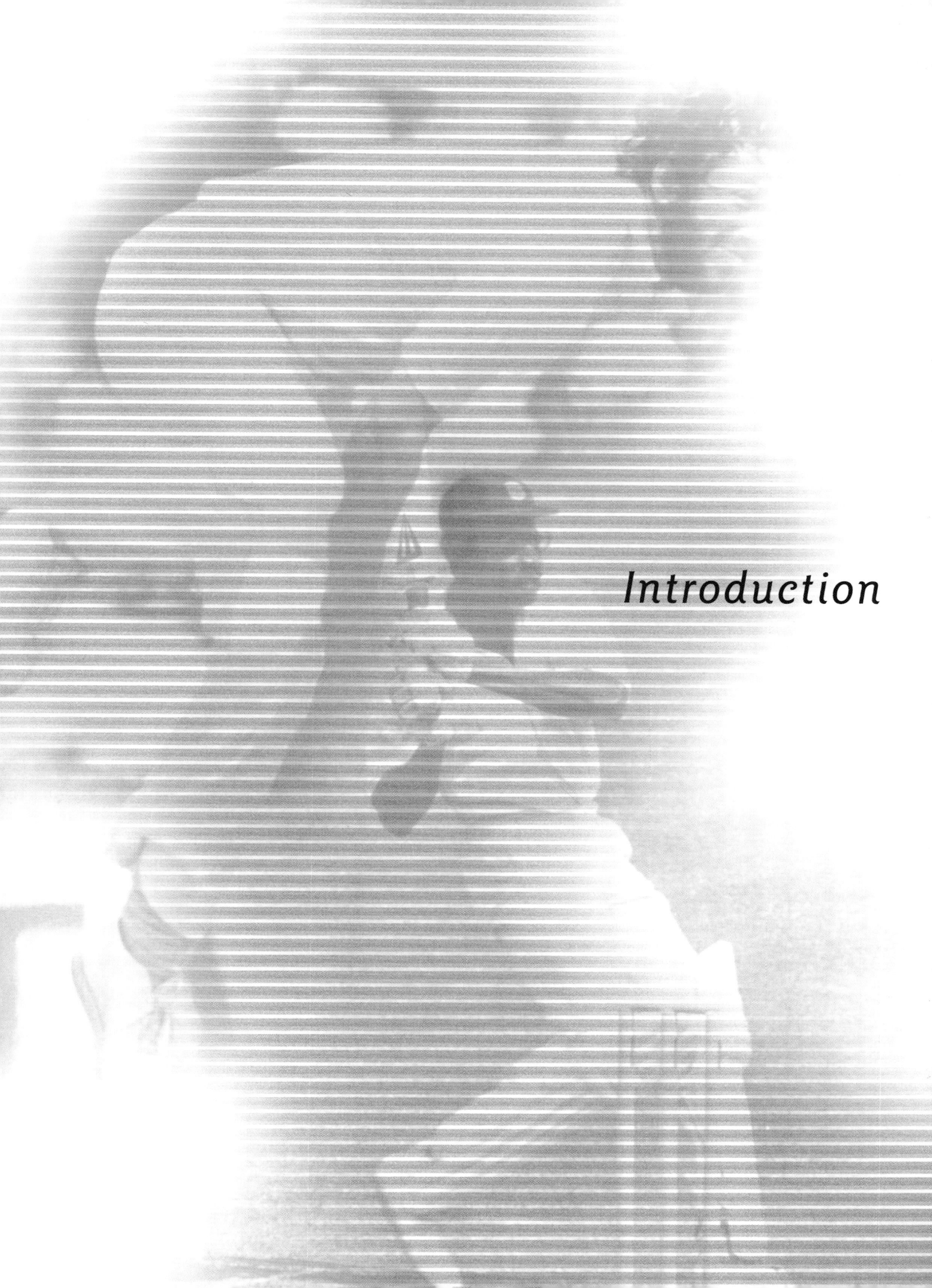

Introduction

At the start of the twentieth century Orville and Wilbur Wright were experimenting with a heavier than air flying machine that could hop about 300 metres in favourable conditions. Less than seventy years later Neil Armstrong was walking on the moon and delivering scripted platitudes to a live television audience. Staggering leaps such as these have made us immune to the pace of change. We accept that new technology will be old by the time it reaches the shops and yet, while researching this book, I was continually struck by the pace at which one-day cricket has developed.

It is less than forty years since the Gillette Cup, the first officially sanctioned one-day competition, saw the light of day. But if we could transport Lance Klusener back in time to play in that competition it would be the sporting equivalent of Mark Twain's Connecticut Yankee in King Arthur's Court. It is not just that one-day cricket has changed in forty years, but that today's professionals are playing a completely different game. What would Ted Dexter, the captain of Sussex at the first Gillette Cup final, have made of fielding circles, floodlights, coloured clothing and all the other things that we have come to take for granted? As we approach the first Cricket World Cup of the new millennium it seems appropriate to look back and take stock.

This is not a scholarly work; it is filled with chauvinistic views, bewildering inclusions and even more bewildering exclusions. I am aware that there are many more pages devoted to batsmen than there are to bowlers, but there is a reason for that. Cricket's authorities have always hated bowlers; it may be that they have never really forgiven their ancestors for adding a middle stump and have been trying to placate batsmen ever since. It was Raymond Robertson-Glasgow, the great 'Crusoe', who pointed out that in cricket the bowlers are the lords, batsmen the commoners and, as with politics, it is not often the lords who get the press. Therefore the few bowlers who have made it into this collection can justifiably be called 'great', which is certainly not true of all the batsmen.

The title of this book, Memorable Moments in One-Day Cricket, is an oxymoron. One-day games happen with such frequency and are in many cases so similar that, far from making indelible impressions on us, moments of high tension that held us spellbound are almost instantly sent to the recycle bin. An incident from the 1983 World Cup final lodged itself in my brain and leapt out after this book was commissioned. India's Balwinder Singh Sandhu had bowled Jeff Dujon of the West Indies with a ball that bounced unusually high, hitting the bottom of the bat as Dujon attempted to lift it out of harm's way, and cannoning on to the stumps.

I remembered it vividly. I could see Dujon's extravagant attempt at playing no shot, his dismay as his wicket fell. I could see Sandhu's pink patka wound tightly around his head and his leap of delight as he realised that another batsman had failed to master his teasing outswing. As a young outswing bowler at the time, of even more modest pace than Sandhu, it was an incident that left a huge impression on me and it was only when I consulted the scorecard that I discovered that the bowler in question was not Sandhu, but Mohinder Amarnath. I had remembered it wrong for twenty years.

A cameraman friend who travels the world covering cricket said that I simply had to include Sanath Jayasuriya's 194 in Sharjah. He vividly remembered the reaction of the crowd when they realised they had been cheated of the first ever double century in one-day cricket. I attempted to look it up but could find no mention of it anywhere. As it turned out the batsman was not Jayasuriya of Sri Lanka, but Saeed Anwar of Pakistan. And it wasn't in Sharjah, it was in Chennai. See what I mean?

Cricket is a game that attracts statisticians. They labour away at recording the game without glimpsing its soul. But the transient nature of one-day cricket demands precise notation, otherwise we all end up remembering things wrong. The scorecards in this book do not lie and they add immensely to the memorable moments hidden within them.

One other apology needs to be made. Most of the games referred to are one-day internationals, an unwieldy term used to describe matches between rival countries. Due to the frequency with which the term has to be used I have shortened it to the unlovely acronym 'ODI'. My old English teacher would be appalled, but there it is. Now read on.

The Birth of One-Day International Cricket

The first one-day international of all was played at the Melbourne Cricket Ground on 5 January 1971. It was a hastily arranged affair, played on the final scheduled day of a rain-aborted Test Match to appease the disappointed public, 46 000 of whom voted with their feet, producing receipts of $33 000.

Both the players and the organisers regarded it as not much more than hit and giggle stuff, but they had underestimated public support for the shorter version of the game. Showing a fine sense of history, it not only took place on the very ground where Test cricket had begun ninety-four years earlier, but also resulted in an Australian victory over England.

Six years later on the same MCG the centenary Test produced a 45-run victory for Australia, the same result as in 1877. The difference this time was that many of the players on either side had

Sussex fast bowler John Snow made a huge impression on the Ashes series in Australia in 1970/71 and when the Melbourne Test was rained out he opened the bowling for England in the first ODI. Gary Sobers is at the non-striker's end, Mike Denness at midwicket in this later match.
(Getty Images/Touchline Photo)

signed letters of intent to join Kerry Packer's breakaway circus, a set-up that wanted to provide a proper living for Test cricketers, but was in the long run more important for its revolutionary treatment of one-day cricket.

Many of the protagonists of the 1971 match were involved in the acrimony of 1977, but they were blissfully unaware as they took the field that history walked with them. Australian captain Bill Lawry won the toss and bucked Test match tradition by inserting the opposition. Lion-hearted paceman Graham McKenzie bowled the first ball, but it was his new ball partner A L 'Froggy' Thomson who took the first wicket.

Geoff Boycott was snapped up by Lawry, having scored 8 runs from 37 balls, almost all of them in singles. Boycott was never a fan of the one-day game, but as a young man scored a brilliant century for Yorkshire in the Gillette Cup final of 1965 and as late as the Ashes tour to Australia in 1983 was dancing down the wicket to the medium pacers to hit them over the top.

England recovered from the early loss of Boycott thanks to a fine innings of 82 from the Surrey left-hander, John Edrich. A dour player in Test cricket, Edrich showed his colleagues the way by scoring his runs off just 119 balls and ended up with the first ever man of the match award. The amount of rain absorbed by the outfield was testimony to the fact that he hit only four boundaries.

Geoff Boycott faced the first ball in ODI cricket, and was also the first wicket to be recorded by the scorers, caught by Bill Lawry off 'Froggy' Thomson for 8. Greg Chappell stands at first slip.
(Getty Images/Touchline Photo)

Australia v England, 1970/71
Melbourne Cricket Ground
5 January 1971 (40-overs match)

Result: Australia won by 5 wickets
Balls per over: 8

England innings
G Boycott c Lawry b Thomson 8
JH Edrich c Walters b Mallett 82
KWR Fletcher c GS Chappell b Mallett 24
BL D'Oliveira run out (IM Chappell/Marsh) 17
JH Hampshire c McKenzie b Mallett 10
MC Cowdrey c Marsh b Stackpole 1
*R Illingworth b Stackpole 1
+APE Knott b McKenzie 24
JA Snow b Stackpole 2
K Shuttleworth c Redpath b McKenzie 7
P Lever not out 4
Extras (b 1, lb 9) 10
Total (all out, 39.4 overs) 190

FoW: 1-21 (Boycott), 2-87 (Fletcher), 3-124 (D'Oliveira), 4-144 (Hampshire), 5-148 (Cowdrey), 6-152 (Illingworth), 7-156 (Edrich), 8-171 (Snow), 9-183 (Shuttleworth), 10-190 (Knott).

Bowling	O	M	R	W
McKenzie	7.4	0	22	2
Thomson	8	2	22	1
Connolly	8	0	62	0
Mallett	8	1	34	3
Stackpole	8	0	40	3

Australia innings
*WM Lawry c Knott b Illingworth 27
KR Stackpole c & b Shuttleworth 13
IM Chappell st Knott b Illingworth 60
KD Walters c Knott b D'Oliveira 41
IR Redpath b Illingworth 12
GS Chappell not out 22
+RW Marsh not out 10
Extras (lb 4, w 1, nb 1) 6
Total (5 wickets, 34.6 overs) 191

DNB: AA Mallett, GD McKenzie, AN Connolly, AL Thomson.

FoW: 1-19 (Stackpole), 2-51 (Lawry), 3-117 (Walters), 4-158 (Redpath), 5-165 (IM Chappell).

Bowling	O	M	R	W
Snow	8	0	38	0
Shuttleworth	7	0	29	1
Lever	5.6	0	30	0
Illingworth	8	1	50	3
D'Oliveira	6	1	38	1

Edrich got good support from Keith Fletcher (24 off 47 balls) and Basil D'Oliveira (17 off 16), but from 124-2 England subsided to 190 all out and were dismissed four balls short of their allocation of 40 overs. As was the case in Australia for more than a hundred years, an over consisted not of six balls, but of eight and in this game the bowlers were restricted to no more than eight overs each.

The ICC spent many years debating how long an ODI should last, so it is intriguing that the organisers of this game came so close first time out. In six-ball terms, 40 eight-ball overs works out to 53.3, just 21 balls more than the 50-over maximum that has become the norm.

Australia's reply was solid, unspectacular and extremely effective, ending in a five-wicket victory with 5.2 overs to spare. Ian Chappell top scored with 60, but spent 103 balls over his runs and the best batting came from the entertaining chain-smoker Doug Walters, who made 41 off 51 balls with six fours.

As a match it did not produce too many fireworks and although Australia played some one-day games against a World XI later that year, it was another eighteen months before the second official ODI took place, between the same two sides at Old Trafford in Manchester during Australia's Ashes tour of 1972.

Surrey left-hander John Edrich scored 82 from 119 balls in the first ODI and ended up with the first ever man of the match award.
(Getty Images/Touchline Photo)

Dennis Amiss, the scorer of the first ODI century, bats in the nets with Gary Sobers among the interested spectators. One of the things Sobers was no doubt contemplating was Amiss' helmet. Amiss was the first Englishman to adopt full head protection (Mike Brearley had worn a skull cap) and with no specialists yet in the market this is clearly a motorcycle helmet. It was heavy and extremely hot and Amiss was the butt of plenty of ridicule at the time, but within two years of this picture being taken helmets were regarded as an essential part of a batsman's armour.
(Getty Images/Touchline Photo)

Two sides of Bob Woolmer: (left) batting for England in a Test match against the West Indies in 1976, four years after he had played in the second ODI as a bowler against Australia. And (facing page) organising practice for South Africa twenty years later, baseball mitt in hand, designer sunglasses on his head and radical ideas in his mind. Woolmer was one of the key factors in South Africa's emergence as the best and most consistent one-day side of the mid-1990s.
(Getty Images/Touchline Photo)

In a taste of things to come, it was the first of a three-match series rather than a one off and England got their rather belated revenge in the first match with a six-wicket win. Among the debutants for England was a man who would become one of the great innovators in one-day cricket as a coach a quarter of a century later – Bob Woolmer.

Woolmer was selected as a medium-pace bowler in this game, a role that he had played for Kent in his early days before his batting developed. It was a further three years before Woolmer made his Test debut and then it was as an upper-order batsman whose stylish cover drives were favourably compared to his Kent colleague, Colin Cowdrey.

Two decades later Woolmer was appointed as the coach of South Africa and he took them to the World Cups of 1995 and 1999. He must take a lot of the credit for developing the team's uninhibited style in the aftermath of the rather one-dimensional tactics that prevailed under the captaincy of Kepler Wessels.

In particular, Woolmer encouraged the batsmen to express themselves, and helped to hone the slog/sweep for Hansie Cronjé and the reverse sweep for Jonty Rhodes. He also developed the somewhat controversial practice of bowlers taking the ball in front of the wicket, rather than behind it, when fielding throws from the outfield. He even managed to send Cronjé on to the field at the 1999 World Cup with an earpiece that could receive advice from the coach while the game was in progress, an innovation that the ICC quickly squashed.

Much of Woolmer's methodology would have seemed patent madness to the players at Old Trafford in 1972, where the cricket remained resolutely formal. Woolmer came on as second change and swung the ball effectively enough to take three for 33 in 10 overs, one short of the allocation of 11 allowed in this match of 55 overs a side.

He bowled Ian Chappell for 53, ending a dangerous stand of 59 with brother Greg, and proved to be the most economical of a classic English conditions bowling line-up. Australia were restricted to 222 for eight and a century from Dennis Amiss eased the home side to victory with all of 5.5 overs to spare. Amiss, an opening batsman from Warwickshire, thus became the first ever ODI centurion and he got his runs in refreshing style, off 134 balls with nine boundaries.

It would be many more years before the governing body in England acceded to public demand for more ODIs and the three-match series became the norm there, generally occurring in May as an aperitif to a Test series. But despite English reluctance, there was no stopping an idea whose time had come and four years after the first one-day international eight teams were contesting the first World Cup in England.

Prudential Trophy, 1972, 1st One-day International
England v Australia
Old Trafford, Manchester
24 August 1972 (55-overs match)

Result: England won by 6 wickets

Australia innings
KR Stackpole c D'Oliveira b Greig 37
GD Watson b Arnold 0
*IM Chappell b Woolmer 53
GS Chappell b Woolmer 40
R Edwards run out 57
AP Sheahan b Arnold 6
KD Walters lbw b Woolmer 2
+RW Marsh c Close b Snow 11
AA Mallett not out 6
Extras (b 2, lb 3, nb 5) 10
Total (8 wickets, 55 overs) 222

DNB: DK Lillee, RAL Massie.

FoW: 1-4 (Watson), 2-66 (Stackpole), 3-125 (IM Chappell), 4-156 (GS Chappell), 5-167 (Sheahan), 6-170 (Walters), 7-205 (Marsh), 8-222 (Edwards).

Bowling	O	M	R	W
Snow	11	1	33	1
Arnold	11	0	38	2
Greig	11	0	50	1
Woolmer	10	1	33	3
D'Oliveira	9	1	37	0
Close	3	0	21	0

England innings
G Boycott c Marsh b Watson 25
DL Amiss b Watson 103
KWR Fletcher b Massie 60
*DB Close run out 1
JH Hampshire not out 25
BL D'Oliveira not out 5
Extras (b 1, lb 6) 7
Total (4 wickets, 49.1 overs) 226

DNB: AW Greig, +APE Knott, RA Woolmer, JA Snow, GG Arnold.

FoW: 1-48 (Boycott), 2-173 (Fletcher), 3-174 (Close), 4-215 (Amiss).

Bowling	O	M	R	W
Lillee	11	2	49	0
Massie	11	1	49	1
Watson	8	1	28	2
Mallett	11	1	43	0
GS Chappell	3	0	20	0
Walters	3	1	16	0
Stackpole	2.1	0	14	0

The First World Cup

The Imperial Cricket Conference (ICC) became the International Cricket Conference in 1965 and admitted Ceylon (as Sri Lanka was known prior to independence in 1972), Fiji and the USA as associate members. The following year Holland, Denmark, Bermuda and East Africa joined on the same basis and in 1971 the idea of a World Cup was first mooted.

As former colonies of the British Empire, cricket in East Africa, Fiji and Bermuda was well established and Ceylon had produced at least one cricketer of genuine first class status in Gamini Goonesena, an allrounder who played county cricket for Nottinghamshire after studying at Cambridge University.

It took much longer for the ICC to recognise the status of Holland and Denmark and, as late as the ICC Trophy held in England in 1986, their claims to first class status were overlooked despite the presence of several county cricketers in their teams. At that tournament Denmark opened the bowling with Soren Henrickson (Lancashire) and Ole Mortensen (Derbyshire) and Holland could call on P J Bakker (Hampshire) and Roland Lefebvre (Somerset).

The first ICC Trophy was held seven years earlier in 1979, when fifteen teams came to England to attempt to qualify for the World Cup proper. Fiji and Papua New Guinea travelled over 20 000 miles to play and were greeted by the coldest, wettest weather in the corresponding period since 1722!

But the fixtures were completed somehow; Sri Lanka beat Canada in the final and both teams played in the World Cup later that year. Amongst the associate members one-day cricket was, of course, the norm, and it was with some prompting from their representatives that the tentative plans for the first World Cup became reality.

From the first whispers in 1971 the tournament took four years to mature and was staged in England in 1975. At that time only England, Australia, the West Indies, India, Pakistan and New Zealand had Test status, with South Africa having been banned from international competition following the D'Oliveira affair in 1970.

Somewhat arbitrarily, Sri Lanka and East Africa were invited to make up the numbers of participating countries from six to eight, while Prudential Insurance put up £100 000 in sponsorship money. There were some huge anomalies, with the two non-Test nations being humiliated in most of their games and the great Indian opening batsman Sunil Gavaskar turning the opening match into a farce.

England had thrilled the Lord's crowd by batting first and making the huge total of 334 for four in 60 overs with a second one-day international century from Dennis Amiss (137) as the lynchpin. And, in a tempting vignette that suggested how one-day cricket might develop, Yorkshire fast bowler Chris Old was promoted to number six in the order and blazed merrily away for 51 not out off just 30 balls.

Sunil Gavaskar scored more Test centuries than Sir Donald Bradman and developed into a fine one-day player. But he will, perhaps unfairly, be remembered for an innings of 36 not out from 174 balls against England in the first World Cup. The explanation was that he was playing for a draw!
(Getty Images/Touchline Photo)

In reply India crawled to 132 for three from their 60 overs, with Gavaskar turning a great day into one of monumental frustration for the crowd by carrying his bat for 36 not out from 174 balls. Later in his career Gavaskar became an effective one-day player, but against England he went strokeless for more than three hours.

The unlikely explanation was that India knew they could not make 335 to win and had therefore opted for a draw, apparently blissfully unaware that one-day cricket did not offer them that option.

Ravi Shastri, the Indian allrounder who made his Test debut five years later said: 'Gavaskar took a lot of criticism for that innings, especially from the senior players in the side like (Srinivas) Venkat and Bishen (Bedi), but amongst the Indian public it passed off lightly because no one took one-day cricket seriously back then. If it happened today the guy would get lynched!'

But Gavaskar's go-slow was an isolated example and the 158 000 spectators who attended the fifteen matches played over two weeks mostly got their money's worth. In the second match New Zealand's Glenn Turner scored 171 not out against East Africa, a total that stood for eight years as the highest in ODIs. In game three Dennis Lillee became the first bowler to take five wickets in an innings with five for 34 for Australia against Pakistan.

On 11 June at Headingley, Leeds, the great Indian slow left-armer Bishen Bedi, recorded the spectacularly parsimonious figures of 12-8-6-1 against East Africa, another mark that stood for years. And on the same day at the Oval in London, Sri Lanka lost their match against Australia, but went some way towards winning the war to be considered as credible opponents.

Replying to Australia's 328-5 they managed a highly respectable 276-4, with runs from Sidath Wettimuny (53), Bandula Warnapura (31), Duleep Mendis (32) and Anura Tennekoon (48) – all players who would be instrumental in winning Test status for Sri Lanka a decade later.

Sri Lanka's efforts have been largely forgotten because perhaps the most significant match of the whole tournament was also played on the same day at Edgbaston in Birmingham.

A One-Wicket Thriller in Birmingham

This match between the West Indies and Pakistan is historically important because it produced the first real ODI thriller, a one-wicket win for the Windies off the fourth ball of the final over.

There were other significant aspects of the match, however, including the ODI debuts of two of the greatest players the game has seen, Gordon Greenidge and Javed Miandad. Greenidge was actually qualified to play for England, his parents having moved to Hampshire when he was just eleven years old, but he chose to play for the place where he was born and became the greatest opening batsman ever produced by the West Indies.

Miandad, the Lahore street fighter who fought his way past Pakistan's class-based selection system on sheer talent, was beginning a career that would see him play in five World Cups, culminating in victory under the captaincy of Imran Khan in Australia in 1992.

As a seventeen-year-old prodigy at the inaugural World Cup he was actually regarded as a leg-spin bowler who could bat a bit. In this match he took one for 46 in 12 overs, while as accomplished a pair of Test match leg-spinners as Mushtaq Mohammad and Wasim Raja bowled 2.4 overs between them. Miandad batted at number six and made 24 off 32 balls in the other half of a fine all round performance.

Batting first upon winning the toss, Pakistan made a formidable 266 for seven with half centuries from Majid Khan, Mushtaq and Wasim. The West Indies then collapsed in the face of a hostile opening burst from the Pathan paceman, Sarfraz Nawaz.

Sarfraz was the bowler credited as the first to perfect the art of reverse swing, but his mincing run to the wicket looked for all the world as though someone had tied his bootlaces together. At Edgbaston, however, he was on top of his game and destroyed the top order on his way to four for 44 and the man of the match award.

It was not, though, a match winning performance. The West Indies collapsed to 99 for five before Clive Lloyd calmed matters with a fine half-century, but when he was caught behind off Miandad for 53 (off 58 balls) the Windies were 151 for seven with only the wicketkeeper and bowlers left.

When Naseer Malik bowled Keith Boyce for 7 they were 166 for eight, but with 101 needed and just two wickets left the revival began. First wicketkeeper Deryck Murray got support from Vanburn Holder, the bandy-legged Barbadian swing bowler, in a stand of 37 for the ninth wicket, but Sarfraz came back and got rid of Holder to reduce the Windies to 203 for nine.

Enter Andy Roberts, the young fast bowler who had come to England a year earlier with his fellow Antiguan Viv Richards to look for a job with one of the first class counties. Roberts developed his batting later in his career with Hampshire, but never aspired to better

Prudential World Cup, 1975
Pakistan v West Indies
Edgbaston, Birmingham
11 June 1975 (60-overs match)

Result: West Indies won by 1 wicket

Pakistan innings
*Majid Khan c Murray b Lloyd 60
Sadiq Mohammad c Kanhai b Julien 7
Zaheer Abbas lbw b Richards 31
Mushtaq Mohammad b Boyce 55
Wasim Raja b Roberts 58
Javed Miandad run out 24
Pervez Mir run out 4
+Wasim Bari not out 1
Sarfraz Nawaz not out 0
Extras (b 1, lb 15, w 4, nb 6) 26
Total (7 wickets, 60 overs) 266

DNB: Asif Masood, Naseer Malik.

FoW: 1-21 (Sadiq Mohammad), 2-83 (Zaheer Abbas), 3-140 (Majid Khan), 4-202 (Mushtaq Mohammad), 5-249 (Wasim Raja), 6-263 (Pervez Mir), 7-265 (Javed Miandad).

Bowling	O	M	R	W
Roberts	12	1	47	1
Boyce	12	2	44	1
Julien	12	1	41	1
Holder	12	3	56	0
Richards	4	0	21	1
Lloyd	8	1	31	1

West Indies innings
RC Fredericks lbw b Sarfraz Nawaz 12
CG Greenidge c Wasim Bari b Sarfraz Nawaz 4
AI Kallicharran c Wasim Bari b Sarfraz Nawaz 16
RB Kanhai b Naseer Malik 24
*CH Lloyd c Wasim Bari b Javed Miandad 53
IVA Richards c Zaheer Abbas b Pervez Mir 13
BD Julien c Javed Miandad b Asif Masood 18
+DL Murray not out 61
KD Boyce b Naseer Malik 7
VA Holder c Pervez Mir b Sarfraz Nawaz 16
AME Roberts not out 24
Extras (lb 10, w 1, nb 8) 19
Total (9 wickets, 59.4 overs) 267

FoW: 1-6 (Greenidge), 2-31 (Fredericks), 3-36 (Kallicharran), 4-84 (Kanhai), 5-99 (Richards), 6-145 (Julien), 7-151 (Lloyd), 8-166 (Boyce), 9-203 (Holder).

Bowling	O	M	R	W
Asif Masood	12	1	64	1
Sarfraz Nawaz	12	1	44	4
Naseer Malik	12	2	42	2
Pervez Mir	9	1	42	1
Javed Miandad	12	0	46	1
Mushtaq Mohammad	2	0	7	0
Wasim Raja	0.4	0	3	0

than number nine and Edgbaston in 1975 proved to be his finest hour with the willow.

He and Murray came together in the 46th over with 64 needed at nearly five an over, a rate not often achieved even by top-order batsmen in these early days. They began circumspectly at first, with Murray unsure whether to farm the strike or give some responsibility to Roberts. As the scoreboard ticked over they grew more confident, while back home in the Caribbean time apparently stood still.

The time difference between England and the West Indies meant that as this match played out its fascinating final stanza it was lunchtime in the islands. The match could not be seen on television, even for the few who owned one, so crowds gathered anywhere there was a radio. It was the most exciting broadcast heard in the islands since the tied Test against Australia in 1961 and business simply ground to a halt.

Bit by bit the pair inched towards victory knowing all the time that any mistake meant the end of the game and, quite probably, the end of the tournament for the West Indies. Pakistan captain Majid Khan changed his bowlers in a vain search for the breakthrough, but with Sarfraz and Asif Masood having bowled their 12 overs he found himself all out of strike bowling.

Pervez Mir had three overs left to bowl when the final over came round, with the West Indies needing 3 runs to win, Mushtaq had already bowled two overs for 7, but Majid made the remarkable decision to bring on a new bowler in a last, desperate throw of the dice.

He handed the ball to Wasim Raja, nominally a leg-spinner, but more adept at topspinners and googlies. Four balls later it was all over and the West Indies had won a match that they had seemed certain to lose. It proved to be the wake-up call the team needed and they went through to the final with two comfortable wins, against Australia in the final group match and against New Zealand in the semi-final.

Deryk Murray keeps wicket for the West Indies against England in the fifth test of the 1976 series in England. Murray rescued his side from oblivion a year earlier when he and Andy Roberts put on an unbeaten 64 for the last wicket to beat Pakistan in the most nail-biting match of the 1975 World Cup. Murray finished 61 not out. Here he keeps to the batting of Dennis Amiss, a colleague of his at the English county Warwickshire.
(Getty Images/Touchline Photo)

Gilmour's Match

Despite losing to the West Indies in the group stage, Australia qualified to meet them at Lord's by winning the other semi-final against England in a remarkable encounter on a beast of a wicket at Headingley, known for all time as Gary Gilmour's match.

Gilmour played only five ODIs for Australia and this was the New South Welshman's first appearance at the World Cup. Given the responsibility of the new ball after Ian Chappell had won the toss at Headingley, he simply decimated England with his left-arm swing. At one point England were 37 for seven, and Gilmour finished with six for 14 as they stumbled to 93 all out.

But this game had more twists to come as the England seamers came roaring back to reduce Australia to 39 for six. In both innings the ball seamed all over the place, five players were bowled and eight given lbw. Of the other three wickets to fall, two were caught behind and the other at first slip. The outfielders were there to relay the ball back to the bowler.

Geoff Arnold made the initial breakthrough for England, but it was the great fast bowler John Snow who gave the home side a real chance when he trapped the Chappell brothers lbw for two and four. Then Chris Old bowled Rick McCosker for 15 and produced two more trimmers to account for Ross Edwards (0) and Rodney Marsh (5).

At that point the match looked like it was all over, but Gilmour came in and changed everything. On a pitch where nobody could get the ball off the square (Keith Fletcher got 8 off 45 balls, McCosker 15 off 50) Gilmour chanced his arm and smashed 28 at a run a ball with five boundaries. Doug Walters held firm at the other end and from 39 for six in 18 overs, the pair added 55 in 10 more to win the game by four wickets.

After being named man of the match in this game, Gilmour took five more wickets in the final but, thanks to fitness problems and Kerry Packer, he played only one more ODI for Australia. In some ways he parallels Shahid Afridi who scored the fastest ODI century ever in his first match, but, despite a much longer time in the national side than Gilmour, never approached such heights again.

Left: *Gary Gilmour took six for 14 with the ball in the match against England at the 1975 World Cup, but his batting was an equally important contribution. On a pitch where nobody could get the ball off the square, Gilmour came in at 39 for six and smashed 28 at a run a ball with five boundaries.*
(Getty Images/Touchline Photo)

Prudential World Cup, 1975, 1st Semi-final
England v Australia
Headingley, Leeds
18 June 1975 (60-overs match)

Result: Australia won by 4 wickets

England innings

DL Amiss lbw b Gilmour	2
B Wood b Gilmour	6
KWR Fletcher lbw b Gilmour	8
AW Greig c Marsh b Gilmour	7
FC Hayes lbw b Gilmour	4
*MH Denness b Walker	27
+APE Knott lbw b Gilmour	0
CM Old c GS Chappell b Walker	0
JA Snow c Marsh b Lillee	2
GG Arnold not out	18
P Lever lbw b Walker	5
Extras (lb 5, w 7, nb 2)	14
Total (all out, 36.2 overs)	**93**

FoW: 1-2 (Amiss), 2-11 (Wood), 3-26 (Greig), 4-33 (Hayes), 5-35 (Fletcher), 6-36 (Knott), 7-37 (Old), 8-52 (Snow), 9-73 (Denness), 10-93 (Lever).

Bowling	O	M	R	W
Lillee	9	3	26	1
Gilmour	12	6	14	6
Walker	9.2	3	22	3
Thomson	6	0	17	0

Australia innings

A Turner lbw b Arnold	7
RB McCosker b Old	15
*IM Chappell lbw b Snow	2
GS Chappell lbw b Snow	4
KD Walters not out	20
R Edwards b Old	0
+RW Marsh b Old	5
GJ Gilmour not out	28
Extras (b 1, lb 6, nb 6)	13
Total (6 wickets, 28.4 overs)	**94**

DNB: MHN Walker, DK Lillee, JR Thomson.

FoW: 1-17 (Turner), 2-24 (IM Chappell), 3-32 (GS Chappell), 4-32 (McCosker), 5-32 (Edwards), 6-39 (Marsh).

Bowling	O	M	R	W
Arnold	7.4	2	15	1
Snow	12	0	30	2
Old	7	2	29	3
Lever	2	0	7	0

Clive Lloyd's Century in the 1975 World Cup Final

An action packed fortnight ended at Lord's with a full house of 26 000 (mostly unbiased) spectators for the final between Australia and the West Indies. In perfect midsummer conditions the game began at 11 am and ended at 8.43 pm, an early reminder that 60 overs a side was too many. But the most important aspect of the contest was that it produced a great game of cricket, one that quickly dispelled the bad memories of some of the earlier contests and left the public hungry for more.

Unquestionably, the correct teams had reached the final and Clive Lloyd's magnificent century for the West Indies lent dignity to the occasion. It was an innings that, when all other aspects of the final had been forgotten, went some way towards converting the crustier members of cricket's aristocracy to the charms of the one-day game.

There was a sensational beginning as Roy Fredericks hooked a Dennis Lillee bouncer for six, only to hit his own wicket with his trailing leg as he swivelled around. Three wickets had fallen for 50 before Lloyd ambled out to join Rohan Kanhai.

Kanhai was the elder statesman of West Indian cricket, the bridge between the Sobers era and the decade of pace, when Lloyd captained a West Indies team that carried all before it. At Lord's Kanhai batted in a calm, statesmanlike manner, allowing his captain to play his natural game.

And what a natural game it was! The great Guyanan left-hander thrashed 102 off 85 balls with 12 fours and two sixes in a partnership that set up a formidable total. Lloyd had the crowd on his side, for he was known and loved in England because of his association with Lancashire. He had been a part of the Lancashire teams that dominated one-day cricket in England at the beginning of the 1970s and, in addition to his batting, was a great cover fielder until his knees gave way.

He walked with a stoop and had a shambling manner that concealed a great athlete. Despite the presence of what looked like jam-jar bottom spectacles he also had a wonderful eye for the ball which he dispatched to all points with a three-pound bat that had a handle thickened by up to half a dozen layers of rubber to accommodate his bear-like paws.

Lloyd seemed to save some of his biggest hits for the Oval, across the river Thames from Lord's, in South London. After one of his many knee operations he came back to play for Lancashire against Surrey in a one-day game when still not quite recovered. Unable to do much more than limp between the wickets, he got 80, mostly in boundaries and, with one prodigious smite, hit a ball from Pakistani leg-spinner Intikhab Alam against the gasholder. In another game he swung Robin Jackman into the Archbishop Tennyson High School playground, a hit that the much-travelled Jackman describes as the biggest he has ever seen. The point was that on his day it was more or less impossible to bowl at Clive Lloyd, and Lord's on 21 June 1975 was quite definitely his day.

Right: 'Antigua me come from.' The other player who made Antigua famous, Andy Roberts. In the first World Cup Roberts and Deryk Murray put on 64 runs against all odds to beat Pakistan by one wicket.
(Getty Images/Touchline Photo)

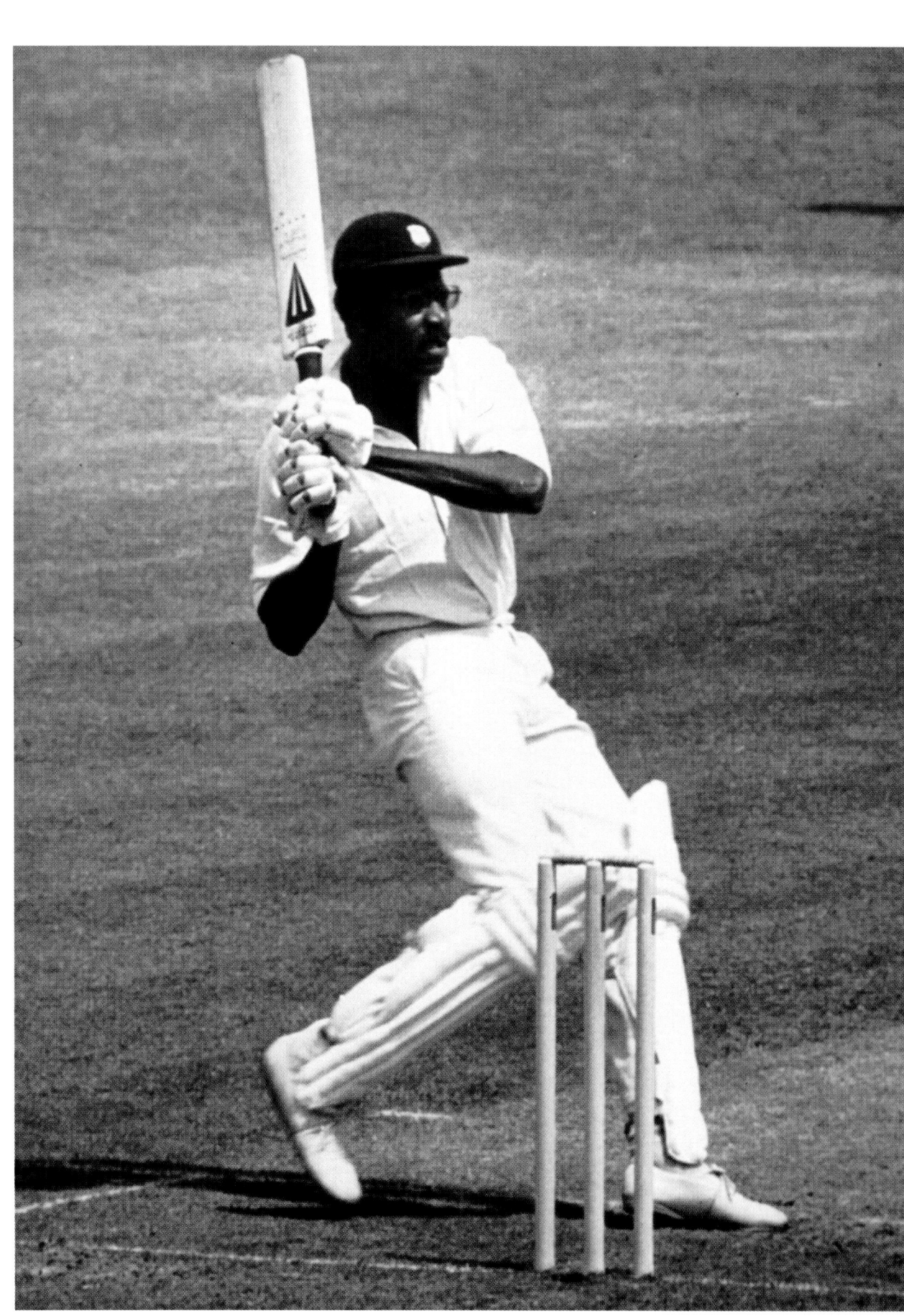

It had nothing to do with the quality of the bowling attack. Australia's team contained their greatest ever fast bowler in Lillee, many people's choice as second best in Jeff Thomson, a bang-in-form Gilmour and the fine fast-medium Max Walker. If anything, they lacked a spinner, but the fifth bowler allocation was competently made up by the medium pace of Greg Chappell and Doug Walters, who between them bowled a respectable 12 overs for 56 runs.

Lloyd did not single out anyone in particular (although Walker's 12 overs cost 71 runs); he just hit whatever came within reach. When Gilmour finally induced an edge to Marsh behind the stumps the partnership was worth 149 and the crisis had been averted. Kanhai, job most emphatically done, went 7 runs later, bowled by Gilmour for an absolutely crucial 55, made from 105 balls. It was a final flourish for the silver-haired former captain. He never played for the West Indies again.

Australia thought they had a chance of wrapping up the innings quickly when the youthful Viv Richards became Gilmour's fourth victim, but from 209 for six the two allrounders Keith Boyce and Bernard Julien put on 52 for the seventh wicket to ensure that Lloyd and Kanhai's heroics had not been in vain. The Windies finished on 291 for eight, a good score, but not an impossible one to overhaul in a tournament that had produced four totals in excess of 300.

Four years later England would be undone by the intimidation factor of the Windies pace attack in the 1979 final, but in 1975 Lloyd could not call on the likes of Joel Garner and Michael Holding. His attack was extremely competent, but not as good (and certainly not as fast) as Australia's.

Andy Roberts was the only genuine fast bowler and he opened the bowling with Julien, a left-arm swing bowler of quixotic moods. Julien came back to England in 1976 on tour with the Windies and played the last of his twenty-four Tests during the series, aged just twenty-six. Several years later, while he should still have been in the prime of his career, Julien was found wandering the shores of Trinidad apparently leading the life of a beach bum.

The first and second change bowlers were Boyce and Vanburn Holder. Both played county cricket and had undergone a familiar transformation from wild fast bowlers to canny medium pacers, the reining in symptoms prompted by the ceaseless travel and playing of cricket in England.

Left: Clive Lloyd smacks another one to the boundary in the 1975 World Cup final. Lloyd's innings of 102 off 85 balls with 12 fours and two sixes gave dignity to the occasion and persuaded a few of the crustier members of the ICC that ODI cricket had a future.
(Getty Images/Touchline Photo)

Prudential World Cup, 1975, Final
Australia v West Indies
Lord's, London
21 June 1975 (60-overs match)

Result: West Indies won by 17 runs
West Indies wins the 1975 Prudential World Cup

West Indies innings
RC Fredericks hit wicket b Lillee 7
CG Greenidge c Marsh b Thomson 13
AI Kallicharran c Marsh b Gilmour 12
RB Kanhai b Gilmour 55
*CH Lloyd c Marsh b Gilmour 102
IVA Richards b Gilmour 5
KD Boyce c GS Chappell b Thomson 34
BD Julien not out 26
+DL Murray c & b Gilmour 14
VA Holder not out 6
Extras (lb 6, nb 11) 17
Total (8 wickets, 60 overs) 291

DNB: AME Roberts.

FoW: 1-12 (Fredericks), 2-27 (Kallicharran), 3-50 (Greenidge), 4-199 (Lloyd), 5-206 (Kanhai), 6-209 (Richards), 7-261 (Boyce), 8-285 (Murray).

Bowling	O	M	R	W
Lillee	12	1	55	1
Gilmour	12	2	48	5
Thomson	12	1	44	2
Walker	12	1	71	0
GS Chappell	7	0	33	0
Walters	5	0	23	0

Australia innings
A Turner run out (Richards) 40
RB McCosker c Kallicharran b Boyce 7
*IM Chappell run out (Richards/Lloyd) 62
GS Chappell run out (Richards) 15
KD Walters b Lloyd 35
+RW Marsh b Boyce 11
R Edwards c Fredericks b Boyce 28
GJ Gilmour c Kanhai b Boyce 14
MHN Walker run out (Kallicharran/Holder) 7
JR Thomson run out (Kallicharran/Murray) 21
DK Lillee not out 16
Extras (b 2, lb 9, nb 7) 18
Total (all out, 58.4 overs) 274

FoW: 1-25 (McCosker), 2-81 (Turner), 3-115 (GS Chappell), 4-162 (IM Chappell), 5-170 (Walters), 6-195 (Marsh), 7-221 (Gilmour), 8-231 (Edwards), 9-233 (Walker), 10-274 (Thomson).

Bowling	O	M	R	W
Julien	12	0	58	0
Roberts	11	1	45	0
Boyce	12	0	50	4
Holder	11.4	1	65	0
Lloyd	12	1	38	1

Boyce's career with Essex was ended by injury a year later, but Holder went on and on with Worcestershire in England and Free State in South Africa. When he gave up county cricket, Holder continued in the minor counties, spending several seasons with Cheshire while playing for Nantwich in the North Staffordshire League. Stumbling upon him in those days he seemed utterly unchanged (he went bald early) apart from a reduction of pace and a waistline several inches closer to the ground, a direct result of legs bandier than John Wayne getting off a horse.

Lloyd, whose respectable slow-medium brought him figures of one for 38 in 12 overs, took up the fifth bowling allocation for the Windies in the final. In the end it may well be the case that Lloyd's bowling, as much as his batting, won the game, for he outperformed Chappell and Walters, who shared the Australian fifth bowler duties by 18 runs. The Windies won by 17 runs.

However, most observers believe that the real difference between the teams was the fielding. Australia's batsmen could cope with the Windies' bowlers, but they were unprepared for the brilliance of their fielding. No fewer than five of the Australians were run out, three of them by Richards, who left no trace on this tournament with the bat, but lit up the final with his panther-like grace in the field.

The two captains meet before the first World Cup final at Lord's in 1975. Ian Chappell of Australia and Clive Lloyd of the West Indies.
(Getty Images/Touchline Photo)

After Boyce had McCosker caught by Alvin Kallicharran for 7, it was Richards who put the skids under Australia as he ran out Alan Turner and the Chappell brothers to knock the stuffing out of the top order. The run-out of Ian Chappell was the key psychological blow, as he was the iron man that Australia looked to for guidance. He had made 62 off 93 balls when he failed to beat Richards' return to bowler Lloyd.

From 162 for three Australia were all but dead and buried an hour later at 233 for nine when last man Lillee joined his fast-bowling partner Thomson at the crease. But both players shared the fast bowler's love of batting and slowly they began to raise hopes in the Australian dressing room. The West Indies players remembered what had happened in the pool game against Pakistan and the nervous tension on the field grew with every over that went by without a wicket.

Just before the end there was a moment of high farce, as Thomson hit a catch to Fredericks off a no-ball. Realising that the catch meant nothing, Fredericks shied at the stumps as the batsmen scrambled a single. He missed, and watched in horror as the ball disappeared into spectators, who had rushed on to the field believing that the match was over when the catch was taken, the no-ball call having gone unnoticed.

Lillee and Thomson then applied law 20 to the situation: 'If a ball in play cannot be found or recovered . . . as many runs as have been completed may be scored'. They ran to and fro hoping to win the match in one hit with the ball lost, but the umpires eventually stopped them and awarded two runs while the ground was cleared. Shortly afterwards the last pair's luck ran out and after a stand of 41, Thomson failed to beat Kallicharran's return to Murray, leaving the Windies victors by 17 runs.

Importantly for the development of ODI cricket this great game was played at Lord's and, in addition to the 26 000 paying spectators, all the significant role players in world cricket were present. It is not inconceivable that had the final been as one-sided as, say, the 1999 final between Australia and Pakistan, there might not have been a second World Cup at all.

But great events tend to throw up great performances from great players and Lloyd's century on the kind of day that English summers bestow but rarely, played in an atmosphere that only Lord's can provide, proved to be the catalyst for the most important development in the game in the last quarter of the twentieth century.

England

Cricket began in England and every significant change to the game has happened there. One-day cricket is no exception. When the game went professional in the nineteenth century county players turned their backs on the one-day game as played in the clubs and villages, and as pitches improved matches lengthened from two to three days. But one-day cricket retained its hold outside the first class arena and as early as 1945 a knockout cup had been recommended as an addition to the county roster.

It eventually came in 1963, sponsored for £6 500 by Gillette, with the seventeen first class counties playing a straight knockout competition of 65 overs per side. It was an attempt to bring the public back to county cricket, for while the post-war boom saw two million people watching charismatic stars such as Dennis Compton, by the end of the 1960s that was down to 300 000. The smaller counties were in danger of going out of business, but one-day cricket changed all that.

The turning point was the decision to play on Sundays, traditionally a day off, or a day to play benefit games. Out of that decision, aimed at getting more people to watch three-day cricket, came the John Player League in 1969, a 40-overs per side competition that has gone through many changes and many sponsors, but still exists to this day. Thanks to the Gillette Cup and Sunday cricket, attendances doubled in short time to 600 000.

Counties who sought the status offered by the new competitions and the money that they brought in looked beyond England for stars from other countries. Two of the first to arrive were the great South African pair of Mike Procter and Barry Richards, who played a season together for Gloucestershire 2nds aged just eighteen before signing full-time contracts, Procter with Gloucestershire and Richards with Hampshire.

Nottinghamshire hired the world's finest allrounder, West Indian Gary Sobers, and within a decade of the first Gillette Cup there were already suggestions from committee men that there were too many foreigners in one-day cricket. But the influx of stars put bums on seats, increased the average player's wages and ultimately laid the foundation for the multimillion dollar industry that ODI cricket has become.

The First Gillette Cup Final

The two sides who made it through to the first Gillette Cup final were Sussex and Worcestershire. Former England opener Don Kenyon led Worcestershire and the current England captain Ted Dexter captained Sussex. It was a gala occasion and for the first time ever Lord's was sold out for a county game before a ball was bowled.

With 65 overs a side allowed, bowlers could deliver as many as 15 overs each, though with both teams dismissed short of their full allocation only Norman Gifford and Mike Buss did so. Gifford, Worcestershire's left-arm spinner who made his England debut a year later, won the man of the match award for an analysis of 15-4-33-4, outstanding figures given the occasion, but also revealing of the tactics employed in the first few seasons of the competition.

John Langridge and Allan Oakman added 62 for the first wicket after Dexter had won the toss, but the introduction of Gifford as second change altered the whole tempo of the match. The openers had prospered against seam, but for many years English players were extremely cautious against good spin and Gifford had more control than most. He took the first three wickets to fall and only a good half-century from England wicketkeeper batsman Jim Parks got Sussex through to a defendable score.

Ted Dexter was born to play one-day cricket. His dashing batting enlivened many a dull Test match and when the Gillette Cup began in 1963, Dexter captained Sussex to the title. Dexter declined to use his own more than useful medium pace bowling in the final, but took plenty of wickets with it in one-day cricket.
(Getty Images/Touchline Photo)

In modern terms, 168 all out from 60.2 overs seems desperately slow, but these were the pioneers. They were familiar with the pace of three-day cricket and, on a soft September day at Lord's with the ball not coming on to the bat, Kenyon set attacking fields, knowing that anything above 150 would give his bowlers a chance.

When Worcestershire replied they found it equally difficult to get the ball away. They were 38 for two when Tom Graveney joined Ron Headley in the middle. Headley was an explosive left-hander, the son of West Indian great George Headley, while Graveney was one of England's greatest ever stylists, who scored more than a hundred centuries in a career that lasted thirty years. These two added 42 largely untroubled runs, but when Graveney was caught in the deep by Dexter off Oakman for 29, the innings went into an irreversible decline.

Defending a smallish score, Dexter had an ace up his sleeve that he employed as soon as the dangerous Graveney was back in the pavilion. Into the attack he brought a twenty-one-year-old fast bowler by the name of John Snow. In 1965 Snow made his Test debut against South Africa, but at Lord's in 1963 he was largely unknown. Snow ripped through the tail with a spell of 8-0-13-3 and effectively clinched the game for Sussex, who thus became the first Gillette Cup champions.

In the years that followed, one-day cricket became the very lifeblood of the game in England, but that didn't mean that the administrators particularly liked it. It was unfairly blamed for many of the ills that befell the England Test team during the 1970s and, perhaps as a result of that, ODI cricket was kept to a minimum for as long as possible. It took the intervention of Kerry Packer, followed by the success of India in the 1983 World Cup, to take ODI cricket to the next level.

Packer's World Series deprived world cricket of a vast number of hugely talented players for two seasons, but the game continued and a generation of young players who would not have progressed quite so quickly in normal circumstances, emerged towards the end of the 1970s. In Australia Allan Border began his prodigious career against Mike Brearley's touring English side in 1978. Brearley's team included the twenty-one-year-old David Gower and the twenty-two-year-old Ian Botham, both of whom saw no distinction between Test and ODI cricket; they just played their natural games.

Left: *John Snow was Ted Dexter's secret weapon in the first Gillette Cup final in 1963. The sixth bowler used by Dexter, a youthful Snow roared in and wrapped up the match with three for 13 in eight overs.*
(Getty Images/Touchline Photo)

Gillette Cup, 1963
Sussex v Worcestershire
Lord's, London
7 September 1963 (65-overs match)

Result: Sussex won by 14 runs

Sussex innings
RJ Langridge b Gifford	34
ASM Oakman c Slade b Gifford	19
KG Suttle b Gifford	9
*ER Dexter c Broadbent b Horton	3
+JM Parks b Slade	57
LJ Lenham c Booth b Gifford	7
GC Cooper lbw b Slade	0
NI Thomson lbw b Flavell	1
A Buss c Booth b Carter	3
JA Snow b Flavell	10
DL Bates not out	3
Extras (b 9, lb 10, nb 3)	22
Total (all out, 60.2 overs)	**168**

FoW: 1-62, 2-67, 3-76, 4-98, 5-118, 6-123, 7-134, 8-142, 9-157, 10-168.

Bowling	O	M	R	W
Flavell	14.2	3	31	2
Carter	12	1	39	1
Slade	11	2	23	2
Gifford	15	4	33	4
Horton	8	1	20	1

Worcestershire innings
*D Kenyon lbw b Buss	1
MJ Horton c & b Buss	26
RGA Headley c Snow b Bates	25
TW Graveney c Dexter b Oakman	29
DW Richardson c Parks b Thomson	3
RG Broadbent c Bates b Snow	13
+R Booth not out	33
DNF Slade b Buss	3
N Gifford b Snow	0
JA Flavell b Snow	0
RGM Carter run out	2
Extras (b 8, lb 9, nb 2)	19
Total (all out, 63.2 overs)	**154**

FoW: 1-7, 2-38, 3-80, 4-91, 5-103, 6-128, 7-132, 8-133, 9-133, 10-154.

Bowling	O	M	R	W
Thomson	13.2	4	35	1
Buss	15	2	39	3
Oakman	13	4	17	1
Suttle	5	2	11	0
Bates	9	2	20	1
Snow	8	0	13	3

David Gower's First ODI Century

Left: *The lazy elegance of David Gower* (Getty Images/Touchline Photo).

Gower's elevation to Test level was, in fact, due to his eye-catching batting in one-day games for Leicestershire. Gower and the former England off-spinner Jack Birkenshaw formed an unlikely left-handed combination at the top of Leicestershire's batting order. Birkenshaw was a gritty northerner who had worked out an effective method of run scoring; Gower was the ghostly slip of a lad who had the priceless gift of natural timing.

Gower was already in prime form when he was selected to play for his country for the first time in an ODI against Pakistan at Old Trafford in May 1978. He batted at number four and caressed 33 off 41 balls in a manner that brooked no argument. When, two days later at the Oval, he scored a masterful 114 not out it was apparent that a great player had arrived on the scene.

During Gower's career the critics were divided on his worth. Those who value style over substance could never understand why his was not the first name on the England selectors' list, the pragmatists argued that he didn't get the number of runs his talent warranted. When he retired in 1993 at the age of thirty-six, Martin Johnson summed up the argument for the former view in Wisden. Johnson wrote about the day that he had first met Gower at pre-season training in Leicester in 1975.

' "Hi there, David Gower", he responded to my introduction and then, in reply to the inevitable follow-up of "What do you do?" he said: "I, um, bat" . . . In retrospect it was like Michelangelo saying that he dabbled in ceilings, or Mozart that he rattled off the odd tune.'

There is an apparently valid argument that his Test match average of 44.25 is that of an underachiever, rather than a great player. Allan Border, for instance, whose career closely followed Gower's, ended with an average of 50.56. However, when you compare Gower's statistics to those of Geoffrey Boycott, one of Gower's most relentless critics and a man held up as the paradigm of responsibility at the crease, the argument does not hold water. Boycott played 108 Tests to Gower's 117, scored 8114 runs to Gower's 8231 and ended with an average of 47.72, or roughly three and a half runs more per innings.

If cricket were baseball, the above comparison would be deemed irrelevant for in America the statistic is king. But cricket is not baseball; it is a game in which aesthetics mean a lot. It is an oft-repeated line among pragmatists: 'It's not how, it's how many'. But with David Gower it was quite definitely the other way round. He made beguiling 30s when Boycott and Border ground out hundreds. He slashed bad balls to slip when Boycott and Border disdainfully watched them go past.

Boycott and Border were the bedrock of their countries' innings for many years and their wickets were prized above all others. Gower was indeed a dilettante by comparison, albeit one who made many vital runs for England. But Boycott and Border were for England and Australia, Gower was for the whole world and when he got out a little of the game died with him.

At the Oval in 1978 Gower played much as he played for his whole career. He never rushed, never belted the ball, and indeed only hit six fours, yet he scored 114 not out off 122 balls. He put on a stand of 105 with the Surrey right-hander Graham Roope, a man who knew the Oval pitch like the back of his hand, and a man who could contribute only 35 off his own bat. When Roope got out, Gower and Ian Botham batted together for the first time in their careers. It didn't last long: Botham was bowled for a single, but those who saw it knew that it would not be the last time those two would bat together for their country.

Left: Batting was easy for David Gower and watching Gower bat was easy for lovers of the game.
(Getty Images/Touchline Photo)

Prudential Trophy, 1978, 2nd One-day International
England v Pakistan
Kennington Oval, London
26 May 1978 (55-overs match)

Result: England won by 94 runs

England innings
D Lloyd b Wasim Raja 34
B Wood b Sarfraz Nawaz 8
CT Radley b Liaqat Ali 13
DI Gower not out 114
GRJ Roope c Naeem Ahmed b Mudassar Nazar .. 35
IT Botham b Mudassar Nazar 1
G Miller lbw b Sikander Bakht 0
CM Old not out 25
Extras (b 5, lb 9, nb 4) 18
Total (6 wickets, 55 overs) 248

DNB: †RW Taylor, JK Lever, *RGD Willis.

FoW: 1-27 (Wood), 2-60 (Radley), 3-83 (Lloyd), 4-188 (Roope), 5-194 (Botham), 6-195 (Miller).

Bowling	O	M	R	W
Sarfraz Nawaz	11	2	48	1
Liaqat Ali	11	1	41	1
Sikander Bakht	11	0	53	1
Wasim Raja	6	0	14	1
Naeem Ahmed	10	0	43	0
Mudassar Nazar	6	0	31	2

Pakistan innings
Mudassar Nazar c Willis b Botham 56
Sadiq Mohammad c & b Old 9
Arshad Pervez lbw b Miller 3
Javed Miandad b Old 0
Haroon Rashid st Taylor b Miller 20
Wasim Raja c sub b Lloyd 44
*†Wasim Bari c Taylor b Wood 1
Sarfraz Nawaz c Gower b Wood 12
Naeem Ahmed not out 0
Sikander Bakht not out 0
Extras (b 1, lb 7, w 1) 9
Total (8 wickets, 55 overs) 154

DNB: Liaqat Ali.

FoW: 1-27 (Sadiq Mohammad), 2-38 (Arshad Pervez), 3-39 (Javed Miandad), 4-80 (Haroon Rashid), 5-117 (Mudassar Nazar), 6-130 (Wasim Bari), 7-154 (Wasim Raja), 8-154 (Sarfraz Nawaz).

Bowling	O	M	R	W
Willis	9	1	25	0
Old	11	1	26	2
Miller	11	3	24	2
Botham	11	2	36	1
Lever	7	1	17	0
Wood	4	0	14	2
Lloyd	2	1	3	1

Botham's international career had begun two seasons earlier and, in common with Gower, his first game was an ODI. It was against Clive Lloyd's magnificent West Indies at Scarborough on the east coast of Yorkshire. Botham made a single in England's total of 202 for 8, dismissed by another man making his ODI debut, Michael Holding. When the Windies batted he was the fifth bowler used and went for 26 in his three overs, but did get the wicket of the gifted Lawrence Rowe.

It was an inauspicious debut and he did not play in the three-match ODI series against Greg Chappell's Australians the following year. But Botham had his revenge when he made his Test debut at Trent Bridge the same year, bowling Chappell in his first over on his way to five for 74.

Botham's selection was due in part to his all-round performance against the Australians for Somerset back in May. Botham had taken wickets and scored runs in a seven-wicket win for the home side at Bath and, as a seventeen-year-old schoolboy, I was fortunate enough to be there for all three days.

As with Gower, it was style above content with Botham. In those days he was not allowed in the slip cordon and instead patrolled the boundary, slinging the ball in with a terrific arm. His bowling was on the fast side of medium and he had a natural outswinger, but it was his batting that really caught the eye. In the first Somerset innings he made 59 and took 24 off an over from the Australian leg-spinner Kerry O'Keefe with two sixes and three fours. The moment that marked Botham as something out of the ordinary came during that over when he jumped down the pitch to drive, slipped, and from a kneeling position cut O'Keefe for four.

When England toured Pakistan and New Zealand later in 1977, a third future England captain made his debut, Mike Gatting. If Gower and Botham were players who saved their best for the international stage, then Gatting was one who all too rarely translated his county form into Test match runs. He was prone to moments of madness where he would lift his bat majestically, only to watch in horror as the off stump cartwheeled out of the ground, or the umpire's finger rose inexorably skywards to confirm an lbw shout. But every time he was dropped he would go back to Middlesex, make mountains of runs and force the selectors to look at him one more time. By 1987 when both Gower and Botham had tried and failed to make a fist of captaining England, Gatting found himself in charge of the England team that went to the 1987 World Cup.

Ten years later, Botham had undergone a back operation and had put on a good deal of weight. He had lost his pace, but it was an inspired move to select him for the 1992 World Cup as his new-found control and undimmed competitive spirit were instrumental in propelling England to the final.
(Getty Images/Touchline Photo)

Left: *Ian Botham in his mighty prime, bowling out the Aussies in the 1981 Ashes series in England.*
(Getty Images/Touchline Photo)

Mike Gatting's Disastrous Reverse Sweep

In the wake of India's momentous win in the 1983 World Cup, the ODI game took off in Asia to such an extent that the ICC finally agreed to hold the 1987 tournament away from England. It was ironic, then, that the final should be between England and Australia, two sides that had never shown any great desire to tour on the subcontinent.

Incredible as it seems in retrospect, the England selectors could find no room in their squad for either Botham or Gower, although the fact that they reached the final seems to vindicate the policy. In the semi-final Graham Gooch had played one of the great World Cup innings, literally sweeping to a century that put India out of the tournament. It transpired that Gooch had decided that the Indian spinners were susceptible to the sweep shot and had practised nothing else in the days leading up to the match.

Australia had progressed by beating Pakistan in the other semi-final, the two results depriving the tournament of its dream final between India and Pakistan in Calcutta. Australia had a well-balanced side, but even they had to admit that good fortune favoured them throughout the tournament.

In Australia's opening group fixture in Madras, India, chasing 270 for six, were dismissed on the penultimate ball for 269, a one-run victory that was the closest margin in World Cup history until 1999. A week later, in a rain-reduced match, they edged past New Zealand by three runs, later won their semi-final by 18, and in the closest final in tournament history defeated England by seven runs. England were narrow favourites going into the final, but things went Australia's way from the moment Allan Border won the toss. Australia made a very respectable 253 for five, all the batsmen made runs and England's decision to play two off-spinners was not vindicated with both John Emburey and Eddie Hemmings going at four and a half an over and posing little threat to players well set.

Even so, in benign conditions it was not an unbeatable score and after losing Tim Robinson to the third ball of the innings, lbw to Craig McDermott, England built a solid platform for the chase. Gooch and Bill Athey put on 65 for the second wicket and when Gooch fell lbw to Simon O'Donnell for 35, the other big gun in the team, Gatting, joined Athey for a second impressive stand. In a vain attempt to break the stand Border had used all five of his front line bowlers to no avail, and with 20 overs remaining England needed six an over with eight wickets in hand, an immensely powerful position on a blameless pitch.

Border had seen the limited effectiveness of the English spinners and his own off-spinner Tim May had gone for 27 in four overs. In retrospect it seems like a stroke of genius, but Border's decision to bowl himself was forced upon him. He had gone into the match with four specialist bowlers and an allrounder (Steve Waugh).

Right: *The moment that lost the 1987 World Cup. England captain Mike Gatting was 41 not out, England were cruising at 135 for two. In desperation Allan Border brought himself on to bowl slow left-arm. Gatting's reverse sweep looks perfectly controlled in this picture, but it wasn't. The ball hit the top edge and looped gently into the hands of Greg Dyer who, in this picture, hasn't yet located the ball or his moment in history.*
(Getty Images/Touchline Photo)

When his five designated bowlers had failed to break the Athey/Gatting stand, his only option was to bring his own left-arm spin to the party.

Border had bowled 25 overs in Australia's seven previous matches at the tournament, picking up four wickets, but going at five an over. He had been playing international cricket for a decade, but this was his most nerve-racking moment. He spent a long time setting his field and then came in to bowl to Gatting with the England captain well set on 41, made from just 45 balls.

What happened next horrified watching England fans, but those familiar with Gatting's inconsistencies understood it in context. This time, instead of playing no shot and falling to a straight ball, Gatting had decided to play the riskiest shot of all, the reverse sweep. There was no guile in the delivery, but it was Border's first: one of cricket's first principles is that you have a look at the bowler before you decide how to play him. Instead Gatting went down on one knee and attempted to backhand it behind point, down to the vacant third man boundary. He got the shot wrong, top edged it and had to watch, mortified, as wicketkeeper Greg Dyer sauntered across to complete the catch.

If Gatting could have one moment back from his career it would surely be this one. If he had stayed still and played the ball on its merits he might have won the game off Border's bowling, rather than losing it. Instead Border stayed in the attack and finished with two for 38 from seven overs.

Oh no, what have I done? Mike Gatting is about to begin the long slow walk back to the pavilion, wicketkeeper Greg Dyer is about to be engulfed by his team mates.
(Getty Images/Touchline Photo)

In the greater scheme of things it shouldn't have mattered. Athey was still in, there was good batting to come and, crucially, there were plenty of overs left. But it was a dismissal that came at a key psychological moment. Although Allan Lamb came in and made a fluent 45 off the same number of balls, Gatting's dismissal forced Athey into his shell and he used up valuable time before falling for 58 made off 103 balls with just two fours.

Some late hitting from Philip DeFreitas took England close, but the penultimate over from Waugh only conceded two runs and that made the task too great for Neil Foster and Gladstone Small.

Thus far, this is as close as England have come to winning the World Cup, although they have appeared in three finals. In 1979 they were blown away by a great West Indies team; in 1992 they ran into an indomitable Pakistan; but in 1987, thanks to Mike Gatting's moment of madness, they came close to beating themselves and that is the hardest thing of all to bear.

Allan Border is mobbed after the fact. The skinny fellow heading for the party is Bruce Reid, the left-arm paceman who once conceded 18 to the flashing blade of Allan Lamb in the final over of a match as England won in improbable fashion in Sydney.
(Touchline Photo)

Reliance World Cup, 1987/88, Final
Australia v England
Eden Gardens, Calcutta
8 November 1987 (50-overs match)

Result: Australia won by 7 runs
Australia wins the 1987/88 Reliance World Cup

Australia Innings
DC Boon c Downton b Hemmings 75
GR Marsh b Foster 24
DM Jones c Athey b Hemmings 33
CJ McDermott b Gooch 14
*AR Border run out (Robinson/Downton) 31
MRJ Veletta not out 45
SR Waugh not out 5
Extras (b 1, lb 13, w 5, nb 7) 26
Total (5 wickets, 50 overs) 253

DNB: SP O'Donnell, +GC Dyer, TBA May, BA Reid.

FoW: 1-75 (Marsh), 2-151 (Jones), 3-166 (McDermott), 4-168 (Boon), 5-241 (Border).

Bowling	O	M	R	W
DeFreitas	6	1	34	0
Small	6	0	33	0
Foster	10	0	38	1
Hemmings	10	1	48	2
Emburey	10	0	44	0
Gooch	8	1	42	1

England innings
GA Gooch lbw b O'Donnell 35
RT Robinson lbw b McDermott 0
CWJ Athey run out (Waugh/Reid) 58
*MW Gatting c Dyer b Border 41
AJ Lamb b Waugh 45
+PR Downton c O'Donnell b Border 9
JE Emburey run out (Boon/McDermott) 10
PAJ DeFreitas c Reid b Waugh 17
NA Foster not out 7
GC Small not out 3
Extras (b 1, lb 14, w 2, nb 4) 21
Total (8 wickets, 50 overs) 246

DNB: EE Hemmings.

FoW: 1-1 (Robinson), 2-66 (Gooch), 3-135 (Gatting), 4-170 (Athey), 5-188 (Downton), 6-218 (Lamb), 7-220 (Emburey), 8-235 (DeFreitas).

Bowling	O	M	R	W
McDermott	10	1	51	1
Reid	10	0	43	0
Waugh	9	0	37	2
O'Donnell	10	1	35	1
May	4	0	27	0
Border	7	0	38	2

West Indies

If Sir Frank Worrell was the man credited with first making the West Indies play as a team, then Clive Lloyd was the man who gave them their killer instinct. He it was who tore up the idea of playing a balanced bowling attack and replaced it with a four-man pace barrage. Once he had convinced the selectors on that issue everything else fell into place and the Windies went on to dominate world cricket for a decade.

But it did not happen overnight. Lloyd's team of young lions had four months to celebrate their victory in the 1975 World Cup before they arrived in Australia as a replacement attraction for the cancelled tour by South Africa. Lloyd wrote before the tour: 'There is basically not much between the two teams where talents and skills are concerned, and you don't need a crystal ball to predict the outcome could hang on a slender thread.' What actually happened, however, was that Australia won the series 5-1.

The difference between the teams lay in the pace bowling department. Australia blasted away with Lillee, Thomson and Gilmour and, under the threat of physical harm, the Windies fell apart. Almost all the major batsmen were hit about the face and body at one time or another – Alvin Kallicharran had his nose broken by Lillee in Perth, Julien's thumb was cracked when he was used as an opener, and Lloyd and Michael Holding were forced to retire hurt in Sydney.

Lloyd was deeply upset by the performance of his team and set about rectifying matters for the tour of England later in 1976. Holding had been blooded in Australia at the age of twenty-one and when both he and Roberts had been fit they had been able to fight fire with fire. For the tour to England Lloyd was given another raw young paceman, Wayne Daniel, and with three quick bowlers to call on, together with a batting line-up that seemed to mature overnight, the Windies simply ran riot.

They became the dominant force in world cricket and an apparently endless supply of fast bowlers began to emerge. Joel Garner, Colin Croft, Malcolm Marshall, Sylvester Clarke and Patrick Patterson all made their debuts over the next few years giving Lloyd an embarrassment of riches from which to choose. And having discovered the key to success in Test cricket he saw no reason to change anything in the one-day game.

Holding, in at the birth of the new era, said: 'In the early days of one-day cricket the West Indies had no real strategy. We pretty much turned up and treated each game as if it were a Test match. Clive Lloyd used to start the game with very aggressive fields and he would only relax them if we didn't get early wickets.

'The tactics that you see being employed now just weren't thought of in those days, it was a completely different game. We went out there to bowl the opposition out, not to try to restrict them. If that team had played in today's scenario we would have played a totally different kind of game, but I think the results would have been the same because we had an outstanding squad of players.'

By the time the 1979 World Cup came around that squad included Desmond Haynes, a young Barbadian opening batsman who was blooded in World Series Cricket. Haynes joined Gordon Greenidge at the top of the order and they became the most successful opening pair in Test and ODI history. They were perfectly matched: Greenidge had an immaculate defensive technique and a withering square cut; Haynes loved to pull and hook and as he grew older developed the best cover drive in the business.

Together they ensured the Windies almost always had a good start on which Viv Richards and Lloyd could build. Their consistency opened the way for Lloyd to select teams that frequently seemed desperately unbalanced, but which inevitably did the job.

Desmond Haynes (left) and Gordon Greenidge, the great West Indian opening pair equally at home in Test and ODI cricket.
(Getty Images/Touchline Photo)

The 1979 World Cup Final

This match was a classic example of West Indian self-reliance. The team consisted of just five batsmen (Greenidge, Haynes, Richards, Kallicharran and Lloyd), an allrounder of no great pedigree (Collis King), a wicketkeeper coming to the end of his career (Deryck Murray), and four fast bowlers (Holding, Roberts, Garner and Croft).

Lloyd's gamble was that the top five would get enough runs to disguise the deficiencies of the lower order and that, whatever happened, his fast bowlers would destroy the opposition. It was a gamble that came perilously close to embarrassing defeat. Put in to bat by England captain Mike Brearley, four of the top five failed, Murray made five and the four fast bowlers did not contribute a run between them. And yet the Windies scored 286 for nine in their 60 overs, just five runs fewer than they had managed in the 1975 final.

In 1975 the Windies were 50 for three when Lloyd came in to turn the match on its head; in 1979 when he was caught and bowled by Chris Old for 13, the score was 99 for four and, with the ball moving around, only Richards survived of the specialist batting. He was joined at the crease by twenty-eight-year-old Barbadian allrounder Collis King, a man described by Holding thus: 'Collis wasn't a great player, but he was a very handy player who bowled good medium pace and could contribute with the bat.'

On this particular day at Lord's, King's contribution was somewhat exceptional: 86 runs off 66 balls with ten fours and three sixes. He added 139 for the fifth wicket with Richards, whom he totally overshadowed with the force of his hitting. Only when King was finally caught in the deep off the left-arm spin of Phil Edmonds did Richards begin to dominate, scoring the vast majority of the remaining 52 runs himself.

He ended the innings in magisterial style by playing a shot that only he was capable of, walking across to the off-side and, with a straight bat, hitting a good length ball from Mike Hendrick into the mound stand at square leg. Some years later I asked Hendrick about that Richards shot and he was still in denial. He would only say: 'I 'ad 'im plumb lbw before he had 10', and that was that.

'Viv scored a great hundred,' said Holding, 'but it was Collis King's innings that swung the game in our favour.' King was particularly severe on England's occasional bowlers, the one Achilles' heel in Brearley's team. The new ball was shared by the fast-medium Hendrick and Ian Botham, England's greatest ever allrounder. Old came on first change and Edmonds bowled his 12 overs for 40 runs with two wickets. The fifth bowler allocation was shared between Graham Gooch, Wayne Larkins and Geoff Boycott, all on the slow side of medium pace, with only Gooch a regular performer at county level.

Prudential World Cup, 1979, Final
England v West Indies
Lord's, London
23 June 1979 (60-overs match)

Result: West Indies won by 92 runs
West Indies wins the 1979 Prudential World Cup

West Indies innings
CG Greenidge run out (Randall) 9
DL Haynes c Hendrick b Old 20
IVA Richards not out 138
AI Kallicharran b Hendrick 4
*CH Lloyd c & b Old 13
CL King c Randall b Edmonds 86
+DL Murray c Gower b Edmonds 5
AME Roberts c Brearley b Hendrick 0
J Garner c Taylor b Botham 0
MA Holding b Botham 0
CEH Croft not out 0
Extras (b 1, lb 10) 11
Total (9 wickets, 60 overs) 286

FoW: 1-22 (Greenidge), 2-36 (Haynes), 3-55 (Kallicharran), 4-99 (Lloyd), 5-238 (King), 6-252 (Murray), 7-258 (Roberts), 8-260 (Garner), 9-272 (Holding).

Bowling	O	M	R	W
Botham	12	2	44	2
Hendrick	12	2	50	2
Old	12	0	55	2
Boycott	6	0	38	0
Edmonds	12	2	40	2
Gooch	4	0	27	0
Larkins	2	0	21	0

England innings
*JM Brearley c King b Holding 64
G Boycott c Kallicharran b Holding 57
DW Randall b Croft 15
GA Gooch b Garner 32
DI Gower b Garner 0
IT Botham c Richards b Croft 4
W Larkins b Garner 0
PH Edmonds not out 5
CM Old b Garner 0
+RW Taylor c Murray b Garner 0
M Hendrick b Croft 0
Extras (lb 12, w 2, nb 3) 17
Total (all out, 51 overs) 194

FoW: 1-129 (Brearley), 2-135 (Boycott), 3-183 (Gooch), 4-183 (Gower), 5-186 (Randall), 6-186 (Larkins), 7-192 (Botham), 8-192 (Old), 9-194 (Taylor), 10-194 (Hendrick).

Bowling	O	M	R	W
Roberts	9	2	33	0
Holding	8	1	16	2
Croft	10	1	42	3
Garner	11	0	38	5
Richards	10	0	35	0
King	3	0	13	0

Déjà vu. Clive Lloyd lifts the World Cup for the second time after the West Indies beat England in the 1979 final. From left, Geoff Boycott (in blazer), Phil Edmonds, Wayne Larkins, Clive Lloyd, Ian Botham, Bob Taylor, Graham Gooch, Malcolm Marshall, Mike Hendrick, Mike Brearley, Viv Richards, Larry Gomes, Chris Old.
(Getty Images/Touchline Photo)

Left: *Collis King transformed the 1979 World Cup final with a violent display of hitting that completely overshadowed his batting partner, the great Viv Richards. With the West Indies precariously poised at 99 for four, King blasted 86 runs off 66 balls with 10 fours and three sixes.*
(Getty Images/Touchline Photo)

King's onslaught showed the England selectors the folly of their selection. Fearing the West Indies pace attack they picked Larkins to bat at number seven where he was unlikely to make much contribution, whatever the circumstances. If they had been bolder in their choice and gone for, say, the left-arm seam of John Lever, the Richards/King stand might never have occurred and the Windies might have been blasted out for less than 200.

But that kind of speculation is easy in retrospect, for, as Holding pointed out: 'We always tended to have the upper hand psychologically in those days and the bowlers always believed that it didn't really matter what total the batsmen got. We always felt that if we made 150 we would bowl the opposition out for 149 and, anyway, at Lord's, Collis' innings meant that we had a good score to defend.'

The only hope for England chasing such a large total was to get a good start and they managed to do that, but at great cost. Said Holding: 'Boycott and Brearley got in, but they were only scoring at about 2 an over and when they got out there was too much pressure on the middle order.'

It was not a unique phenomenon in those days. With courage and a slice of good fortune, good players could stay in against the Windies pace attack, but in ODI cricket something more was needed and was rarely forthcoming. In the semi-final the Windies had beaten Pakistan by 43 runs, despite a stand of 166 between Majid Khan and Zaheer Abbas.

Pakistan's master batsman, Zaheer Abbas is one of only five non-Englishmen to score more than a hundred first class centuries. But even he could not master the West Indies attack of 1979.
(Getty Images/Touchline Photo)

These two were among the finest batsmen in the world at the time. Zaheer, a wonderful stylist who played many seasons for Gloucestershire in the county championship, ended his career with 108 centuries and both he and Majid had prospered in World Series Cricket. But on a blameless pitch at the Oval they found, like Brearley and Boycott subsequently, that you could get in against the Windies attack, but you could not get on top of it.

England's opening pair were a good deal more limited than Majid and Zaheer and they used up too many overs in putting on 129. And that was disappointing because the middle order of Derek Randall, Gooch, David Gower and Botham was as good a line-up as England had had for twenty years and, given a reasonable time to play themselves in, may have made a difference, but as Holding recalled: 'They got out to shots they shouldn't have played against Joel Garner.'

Garner and Croft were the executioners who picked up the last eight wickets for 11 runs and had it not been for Richards' century Garner's five for 38 would surely have won the man of the match award. Known as 'Big Bird' after the character in Sesame Street, Garner was 6 foot 8 and possessed the most devastating Yorker in the game. He clean bowled Gooch, Gower, Larkins and Old and had Bob Taylor caught behind.

Said Holding: 'Joel always had a great Yorker and in one-day cricket he could pretty much bowl it at will. The only time I ever saw anybody get on top of Joel was Imran Khan in Sharjah, but the Sharjah pitch was so good that it was almost understandable.'

Having defended their title, the Windies came back to England a year later and destroyed them in the Test series. They were apparently at their peak, which made it even harder for English supporters to bear when they came back again in 1984 and did it all over again with an even better team.

Right: *The Big Bird. Joel Garner was six foot eight inches tall and released the ball from about nine feet. Not surprisingly, his Yorker was devastating.*
(Getty Images/Touchline Photo)

Viv Richards' 189 not out at Old Trafford

With the help of his friend, Andy Roberts, Viv Richards put the West Indian island of Antigua on the map in the 1970s and 80s. Richards was an intimidator of bowlers, able to hit the fastest out of the ground, but equally capable of subtle glides such as the one seen here.
(Getty Images/Touchline Photo)

**Texaco Trophy, 1984
England v West Indies
Old Trafford, Manchester**
31 May 1984 (55-overs match)

Result: West Indies won by 104 runs

West Indies innings
CG Greenidge *c* Bairstow *b* Botham 9
DL Haynes run out 1
RB Richardson *c & b* Willis 6
IVA Richards not out 189
HA Gomes *b* Miller 4
*CH Lloyd *c* Pringle *b* Miller 8
+PJL Dujon *c* Gatting *b* Miller 0
MD Marshall run out 4
EAE Baptiste *c* Bairstow *b* Botham 26
J Garner *c & b* Foster 3
MA Holding not out 12
Extras (b 4, lb 2, w 1, nb 3) 10
Total (9 wickets, 55 overs) 272

FoW: 1-5 (Haynes), 2-11 (Greenidge), 3-43 (Richardson), 4-63 (Gomes), 5-89 (Lloyd), 6-98 (Dujon), 7-102 (Marshall), 8-161 (Baptiste), 9-166 (Garner).

Bowling	O	M	R	W
Willis	11	2	38	1
Botham	11	0	67	2
Foster	11	0	61	1
Miller	11	1	32	3
Pringle	11	0	64	0

England innings
G Fowler *c* Lloyd *b* Garner 1
TA Lloyd *c* Dujon *b* Holding 15
MW Gatting lbw *b* Garner 0
*DI Gower *c* Greenidge *b* Marshall 15
AJ Lamb *c* Richardson *b* Gomes 75
IT Botham *c* Richardson *b* Baptiste 2
+DL Bairstow *c* Garner *b* Richards 13
G Miller *b* Richards 7
DR Pringle *c* Garner *b* Holding 6
NA Foster *b* Garner 24
RGD Willis not out 1
Extras (lb 6, nb 3) 9
Total (all out, 50 overs) 168

FoW: 1-7 (Fowler), 2-8 (Gatting), 3-33 (Lloyd), 4-48 (Gower), 5-51 (Botham), 6-80 (Bairstow), 7-100 (Miller), 8-115 (Pringle), 9-162 (Foster), 10-168 (Lamb).

Bowling	O	M	R	W
Garner	8	1	18	3
Holding	11	2	23	2
Baptiste	11	0	38	1
Marshall	6	1	20	1
Richards	11	1	45	2
Gomes	3	0	15	1

The great Michael Holding sending shivers down the spine of another batsman. Holding had no great reputation with the bat, but he once made 12 not out at Old Trafford while, at the other end, Viv Richards played an innings of awesome majesty.
(Getty Images/Touchline Photo)

Whispering death. Umpires said they couldn't hear him coming and this is the moment before Michael Holding hits the crease to unleash another thunderbolt. Holding was a 400 metre runner in his youth and had a mesmerising run to the crease. So much so that England captain Mike Brearley advised players to time Holding's walk back and run and to look up only when he was three strides from the crease. A good idea in theory, but Holding was not averse to coming off a short run now and again, which put players who adopted Brearley's theory in great peril.
(Getty Images/Touchline Photo)

By 1984 the world had become used to West Indian domination. They had lost a number of players to a rebel tour of South Africa, among them Croft and Sylvester Clarke, but it made no difference to the strength of their bowling attack. Malcolm Marshall had made his debut on the 1980 tour as a tearaway fast bowler, but by 1984 he was the master of his trade, every bit as quick as he had been in 1980 and now capable of swinging the ball both ways.

Holding had cut down the majestic run-up of old and was more often fast-medium than genuinely quick, but during the Test match at the Oval when a rare stand of substance had developed for England, he returned to his full run and blasted out three quick wickets to change the match irrevocably. Garner was regarded by most of his contemporaries as the bowler they least liked to face. His great height enabled him to get lift on pitches dead to ordinary mortals, and his Yorker went on and on bamboozling people.

Richie Richardson and Larry Gomes became batsmen of high quality and the emergence of Jeff Dujon as the wicketkeeping successor to Deryck Murray made a huge difference to the balance of the side. Dujon was a genuine batsman who also happened to keep wicket, something that allowed the ageing Lloyd to slip himself down to sometimes as low as number seven.

But as was the case in the 1979 World Cup Final, the top order failed against England at Old Trafford in the first ODI of a three-match series, intended as an appetiser for the Test series. Other than Richards, no one in the top order made double figures and, as was the case in 1979, the great man had to wait for a young allrounder to get support of any kind. This time it was from twenty-one-year-old Eldine Baptiste, who made 26 of a stand worth 59. But when he was out, closely followed by Garner, the Windies were 166 for nine and it seemed that not even Richards could save them this time. Wrong again.

Richards was thirty-two in 1984. His youthful scoring excesses were behind him and he had achieved so much that bowlers felt they had a chance against him, principally because he became easily bored. But, if anything, his mastery was greater in the 1980s because he could turn it on at will. Put simply, if Viv wanted to score a hundred you couldn't stop him. In the whole history of the game there may be half a dozen players of whom that could be said.

He played every shot in the book, but the one that drove bowlers into insane asylums was the flick through midwicket played with a straight bat. He would stretch his front foot across to meet the ball and as he brought the bat into contact with it, his wrists would turn it through a loaded on-side field, usually for four.

Two of England's greatest bowlers, Ian Botham and Bob Willis, played in this game and they both attempted to keep the ball as wide of off stump as the umpires would allow. It made no difference to Richards, who would reach out and smash good length balls through his favourite area. Asked how his son played shots impossible for the best of his contemporaries, Viv's father said: 'My boy got eyes like a pigeon.'

At 166 for nine Holding walked to the wicket to join Richards. What followed was a master class in the art of farming the strike. The pair put on 106 for the last wicket and were still there when the innings came to an end after 55 overs. Of those 106 runs Holding made 12. Eighteen years later he was still in awe of Richards' dominance that day.

He said: 'Viv played so many great innings that it's difficult to say that was the best, but certainly it was very influential as far as the match was concerned. We were in a lot of bother and that partnership and his innings turned it totally in our favour.

Left: *The Master Blaster. Viv Richards had wrists of corded steel that meant that he could whip straight balls through midwicket merely by turning the face of the bat at the moment of impact. It became a game within a game to stop him doing it and bowlers such as Ian Botham and Bob Willis aimed two feet outside off stump. It never worked: Richards would simply reach across with his left leg and clobber the ball past mid-on.*
(Getty Images/Touchline Photo)

Malcolm Marshall didn't have the imposing build of a Michael Holding or a Joel Garner, but he lasted longer than either and took more Test wickets as well. He began as a tearaway fast bowler, but developed into a fast-medium swing bowler with exquisite control. After retiring from international cricket Marshall went as player/coach to Natal in South Africa and had a profound effect on the early development of Shaun Pollock.
(Getty Images/Touchline Photo)

'He was devastating and managed to demoralise the bowlers to the extent that they didn't want to come in and bowl. There was a bit of moisture in the pitch and initially Botham and Willis bowled well and we lost wickets regularly. When I came in Viv said, "Mikey, just survive and stay at the other end."

'That's what I tried to do and Viv didn't allow me to face too many deliveries initially. The most I had to face was two an over, most times it was one and there were times when it was none.'

Statistics bear out Holding's memory. In all, he faced just 27 balls, two of which he hit for four.

'There was no pressure on me because Viv was doing all of the scoring and when we got to the stage where we thought we were safe he started hitting anyone anywhere. It was a pleasure to stand at the other end and watch him, but there was also a bit of danger involved. I couldn't really be backing up too far because the ball was tending to come back quite quickly in my direction!

'The innings lifted our morale, because we were a bit down when the wickets had been tumbling, and it demoralised England. When we went out to field I don't think England really thought they had a chance. That innings had turned the match upside down.'

Richards made 189 not out from 170 balls with 21 fours and five sixes. It remained the highest score in ODI cricket for more than a decade, but more than that, it gave credibility to ODI cricket. Those who were privileged to see it, either at the ground or on television, speak with awe of Richards' innings to this day. It may have been overtaken in the record books, but in terms of aesthetics it will never be superseded.

India

When I was at school one of my set books was *A Passage To India* by E M Forster. On the day that we were to begin our class discussion, the teacher opened up proceedings by asking what we thought of when India was mentioned. 'Curry,' said one; 'erotic art,' said another; 'spin bowling,' said a third. While these responses may reveal more about the obsessions of a group of pubescent teenagers than anything else, the mere fact that spin bowling rated a mention was significant.

These were the 1970s when India had such a dearth of seam bowling that the great opening batsman Sunil Gavaskar would trundle a couple of overs with the new ball in an attempt to rough it up sufficiently to give to one of the spinners. And what spinners they were! Eripali Prasanna, regarded as the finest off-spinner since Jim Laker; Srinivas Venkataraghavan, slower through the air than Prasana, but possessed of almost metronomic accuracy; Baghwat Chandrasekhar, the leg-spinner with the withered arm who could find bounce in the deadest pitch; and my favourite, Bishen Bedi, the most beguiling slow left-armer of all time, a man who would happily give away six boundaries to earn a wicket.

The only trouble was that to be fully effective, the quartet needed plenty of fielders around the bat, not something that sat easily with the crash, bang, wallop of one-day cricket. Accordingly, they left no impression on the first two World Cups and by the time the 1983 version came along they were regarded as something of a hopeless case. And yet twenty years later India, like the rest of Asia, has gone dilly over ODI cricket. They have in Sachin Tendulkar the finest batsman in the world who is equally adept in both forms of the game, and a string of exciting players who have become household names wherever cricket is played. So what happened?

'The '83 World Cup,' says Ravi Shastri, one of India's greatest ever allrounders. 'After that it was a totally different scenario. The interest and enthusiasm for the game in the streets was amazing. In a five-year period we won a lot of tournaments and when you win it has an impact.'

During that period India could call on a number of great players, but one in particular proved to be a talisman for the team: Kapil Dev. When Kapil made his Test debut against the West Indies in 1978 he was just nineteen years old and known as the Haryana Hurricane. It was understandable that after a decade of spin bowling dominance anyone who could propel the ball above medium pace would be talked of in exaggerated terms. Kapil was in fact fast-medium, not genuinely quick, and towards the end of his career he was distinctly slow-medium. But the one thing he had at the outset that he never lost was the ability to swing the ball away from the bat and that, more than anything, gave India a fighting chance.

Right: *Sachin Tendulkar might have made the grade as a bowler if he had not had a divine gift for batting. The only thing that stops him being a consistent wicket taker is his inability to bowl the same ball twice. This looks like the grip for a googly, but with Sachin who knows?*
(Touchline Photo)

Kapil was one of the quartet of allrounders who bestrode the game between the late 1970s and early 1990s. Ian Botham of England, Richard Hadlee of New Zealand and Imran Khan of Pakistan were the others and while they were active, cricket watchers loved to conjecture who was the best of the four. Botham was probably the best batsman, Hadlee unquestionably the best bowler, but in terms of statistics Kapil is at the top of the tree. When he retired in 1994 he had taken a (then) world record 434 Test wickets and scored 5 248 runs.

He always regarded his role in the team as a wicket taker, but if he had never bowled a ball he would have made the Indian team as a batsman. What made him so difficult to bowl to was that he had no particular preference for the front or back foot and was equally adept at playing through the on- and off-side. Those may seem fairly basic attributes, but look around in any era and count the players of whom it can truthfully be said, and you'll discover how rare it actually is.

Kapil seemed to save his best for Lord's. In 1982 he made 89 off 55 balls with 13 fours and three sixes, while in 1990 he was responsible for one of the most audacious pieces of batting the game has ever seen. This was Graham Gooch's match; he scored a triple century in the first innings and another century in the second.

When India replied to England's first innings the last man, Narendra Hirwani joined Kapil with 24 still needed to avoid the follow-on. Recognising a rabbit when he saw one, Kapil decided to settle the issue quickly. He slammed four successive sixes off the bowling of Eddie Hemmings to pass the mark and to prove that Kapil had been right to take the initiative, Hirwani was out to the first ball of the next over.

Kapil rewrote the record books during his extraordinary career, yet his finest moment, the one that he called 'the innings of a lifetime', came against non-Test match opposition in a one-day tournament on an obscure ground in rural Kent.

Facing page: 'All the chances during his innings went into the car park,' Ravi Shastri recalls. A magnificent picture of Kapil Dev in full flow during his innings of 175 not out against Zimbabwe at Tunbridge Wells. In the background you can see in full bloom the rhododendrons for which the ground is famous.
(Getty Images/Touchline Photo)

Kapil Dev's Lone Hand

Cricket had been played at the Nevill Ground since 1898. The original pavilion was burnt down in 1913 during a protest by the suffragettes. On the cricketing front, in 1932 Tich Freeman of Kent and Valance Jupp of Northamptonshire shared 28 wickets of the 30 to fall in the match. But both of those events have been overshadowed by the performance of Kapil Dev during the 1983 World Cup.

Choosing to bat first, India were reduced to 17 for five by some fine pace bowling from Kevin Curran and Peter Rawson. Dave Houghton kept wicket at this stage of his career and took three catches behind the stumps. This was no flash in the pan from Zimbabwe; on the opening day of the tournament they had beaten Kim Hughes' Australian team by 13 runs and with the likes of Houghton and Curran (who played county cricket for Gloucestershire) they had a more than capable unit, particularly in English conditions.

But inevitably a partnership developed and Kapil put on 60 for the sixth wicket with Roger Binny. But Binny was out to the off-spin of John Traicos (then a relatively youthful thirty-five) and one run later Duncan Fletcher had Ravi Shastri caught by Andy Pycroft. India were now 78 for seven and the organisers were worried that the huge crowd that had packed into the ground would have nothing to watch after lunch. Then the fireworks started, as Shastri recalls.

'We were 17 for five and 78 for seven, but Kapil just played his natural game. Not for one moment did he try to defend, he just treated the bowling on merit. It was his day and the ball just kept disappearing into the car park. Unfortunately there were no television cameras there because it was an outstanding exhibition of clean hitting.' (The reason for the lack of television coverage was that the BBC camera crew had gone on strike!)

'Zimbabwe had a good attack and added to that they were an outstanding fielding side. The pitch was a little damp first thing and they exploited it well with movement off the seam. They fielded well, bowled well, but Kapil was just unstoppable. All the chances during his innings went into the car park!'

From a desperate position Kapil hauled his team back into the match. After Binny and Shastri had gone he got good support from Madan Lal, who made 17 of a partnership worth 62 and then wicketkeeper Syed Kirmani kept him company through to the end of the innings at 266 for eight. Their ninth-wicket partnership of 126 remains a record to this day.

As Shastri said, Kapil gave no real chances, except a very difficult one to Grant Paterson on the boundary in the nineties and a number of miscued strokes that fell clear of the fielders. In all, he batted for one minute more than three hours, hit six sixes (mostly over the long boundary – the pitch was on the edge of the square) and 16 fours. He reached three figures from just 72 balls.

Prudential World Cup, 1983
India v Zimbabwe
Nevill Ground, Tunbridge Wells
18 June 1983 (60-overs match)

Result: India won by 31 runs

India innings
SM Gavaskar lbw b Rawson 0
K Srikkanth c Butchart b Curran 0
M Amarnath c Houghton b Rawson 5
SM Patil c Houghton b Curran 1
Yashpal Sharma c Houghton b Rawson 9
*N Kapil Dev not out 175
RMH Binny lbw b Traicos 22
RJ Shastri c Pycroft b Fletcher 1
S Madan Lal c Houghton b Curran 17
+SMH Kirmani not out 24
Extras (lb 9, w 3) 12
Total (8 wickets, 60 overs) 266

DNB: BS Sandhu.

FoW: 1-0 (Gavaskar), 2-6 (Srikkanth), 3-6 (Amarnath), 4-9 (Patil), 5-17 (Yashpal Sharma), 6-77 (Binny), 7-78 (Shastri), 8-140 (Madan Lal).

Bowling	O	M	R	W
Rawson	12	4	47	3
Curran	12	1	65	3
Butchart	12	2	38	0
Fletcher	12	2	59	1
Traicos	12	0	45	1

Zimbabwe innings
RD Brown run out 35
GA Paterson lbw b Binny 23
JG Heron run out 3
AJ Pycroft c Kirmani b Sandhu 6
+DL Houghton lbw b Madan Lal 17
*DAG Fletcher c Kapil Dev b Amarnath 13
KM Curran c Shastri b Madan Lal 73
IP Butchart b Binny 18
GE Peckover c Yashpal Sharma b Madan Lal 14
PWE Rawson not out 2
AJ Traicos c & b Kapil Dev 3
Extras (lb 17, w 7, nb 4) 28
Total (all out, 57 overs) 235

FoW: 1-44 (Paterson), 2-48 (Heron), 3-61 (Pycroft), 4-86 (Brown), 5-103 (Houghton), 6-113 (Fletcher), 7-168 (Butchart), 8-189 (Peckover), 9-230 (Curran), 10-235 (Traicos).

Bowling	O	M	R	W
Kapil Dev	11	1	32	1
Sandhu	11	2	44	1
Binny	11	2	45	2
Madan Lal	11	2	42	3
Amarnath	12	1	37	1
Shastri	1	0	7	0

After reaching his century Kapil called for a new bat, one of the new fashion at that time with tapered-down shoulders and shaped almost like a baseball bat, and stepped up the assault even more. At the close of the innings Sunil Gavaskar, Kapil's rival for the captaincy, met him as he came off the field with a cup of water, a fine mark of respect. His 175 not out stood for twelve months as the highest in ODI cricket, beaten eventually by Viv Richards' 189 against England at Old Trafford.

But Kapil's job was not yet done. After a soak in the bath he went back out to open the bowling as India attempted to defend their score. Zimbabwe began with a good opening stand of 44, but were set back by two run-outs and subsequently slumped to 113 for six. Curran and Butchart put on 55 for the seventh wicket and as long as the former was at the crease there was a chance. But eventually he misjudged the pace of a long hop and lobbed an easy catch off the splice, caught by Shastri off Madan Lal for 73.

Kapil bent down to kiss the ground as he came off the field as the victorious captain and for India the match proved to be the turning point of the tournament, for had they lost to Zimbabwe they would almost certainly have failed to reach the semi-finals. As it was, they went on to win the World Cup, beating West Indies in the final.

Kapil Dev hoists the trophy on the Lord's balcony after India's upset win in the 1983 World Cup final.
(Getty Images/Touchline Photo)

India Wins The World Cup

Having turned their tournament around against Zimbabwe, India reached the final confident of their own ability, but it was not a confidence shared by most of the pundits. In the previous two World Cups India had but one win against East Africa to put next to their list of defeats and when they began the 1983 tournament the bookmakers offered odds of 66-1 on them taking the title. By contrast, the West Indies had won both of the World Cups played to that point and, with players such as Malcolm Marshall and Jeffrey Dujon coming into the team, were significantly stronger than they had been in 1979.

The Indian team that had been dominated by spin bowling in the 1970s was now filled with right-arm medium pacers of whom Kapil Dev was the quickest and Mohinder Amarnath the slowest. Their problem was a lack of variety and any real pace and the only spin option came from Kirti Azad. In the event, Azad only bowled three overs and the Indian medium pacers proved harder to hit than the West Indian pace quartet. But when Clive Lloyd won the toss he was not to know that. He put India in and a familiar collapse set in due to the unrelenting pace barrage provided by Andy Roberts, Joel Garner, Malcolm Marshall and Michael Holding.

Gavaskar went early and only Krishnamachari Srikkanth, with seven fours and a six, took the Windies bowlers on. The rest of the top order all got starts, but no one came close to putting together the long innings that the situation required. When Holding bowled Syed Kirmani for 14 the innings was over at 183 with 5.2 overs unused. The bowlers sat down in the dressing room to relax and watch the batsmen wrap up a hat-trick of World Cups. Before long, however, they were rushing around looking for pads, bats and gloves.

Holding said: 'When we bowled, in my book we had done our job. Perhaps at the end of the entire game we might have looked back and wondered whether we had allowed them to get too many runs, but I don't think on that pitch that 183 was too many.

'There wasn't really a point when we believed we were in trouble, not until it was too late. I think the reason we lost was that we were a little overconfident; we took it for granted that with India only getting 183 we would get the runs and although a couple of wickets went down early everyone in the dressing room just thought there was no way we could lose.

'That's what led to our downfall. I think if we'd woken up a bit earlier to the fact that it was slipping away we could have done something about it. The ball was moving around and I think some of the shots our guys got out to were a little ambitious.'

Prudential World Cup, 1983, Final
India v West Indies
Lord's, London
25 June 1983 (60-overs match)

Result: India won by 43 runs
India wins the 1983 Prudential World Cup

India innings
SM Gavaskar c Dujon b Roberts 2
K Srikkanth lbw b Marshall 38
M Amarnath b Holding 26
Yashpal Sharma c sub (AL Logie) b Gomes 11
SM Patil c Gomes b Garner 27
*N Kapil Dev c Holding b Gomes 15
KBJ Azad c Garner b Roberts 0
RMH Binny c Garner b Roberts 2
S Madan Lal b Marshall 17
+SMH Kirmani b Holding 14
BS Sandhu not out 11
Extras (b 5, lb 5, w 9, nb 1) 20
Total (all out, 54.4 overs) 183

FoW: 1-2 (Gavaskar), 2-59 (Srikkanth), 3-90 (Amarnath), 4-92 (Yashpal Sharma), 5-110 (Kapil Dev), 6-111 (Azad), 7-130 (Binny), 8-153 (Patil), 9-161 (Madan Lal), 10-183 (Kirmani).

Bowling	O	M	R	W
Roberts	10	3	32	3
Garner	12	4	24	1
Marshall	11	1	24	2
Holding	9.4	2	26	2
Gomes	11	1	49	2
Richards	1	0	8	0

West Indies innings
CG Greenidge b Sandhu 1
DL Haynes c Binny b Madan Lal 13
IVA Richards c Kapil Dev b Madan Lal 33
*CH Lloyd c Kapil Dev b Binny 8
HA Gomes c Gavaskar b Madan Lal 5
SFAF Bacchus c Kirmani b Sandhu 8
+PJL Dujon b Amarnath 25
MD Marshall c Gavaskar b Amarnath 18
AME Roberts lbw b Kapil Dev 4
J Garner not out 5
MA Holding lbw b Amarnath 6
Extras (lb 4, w 10) 14
Total (all out, 52 overs) 140

FoW: 1-5 (Greenidge), 2-50 (Haynes), 3-57 (Richards), 4-66 (Gomes), 5-66 (Lloyd), 6-76 (Bacchus), 7-119 (Dujon), 8-124 (Marshall), 9-126 (Roberts), 10-140 (Holding).

Bowling	O	M	R	W
Kapil Dev	11	4	21	1
Sandhu	9	1	32	2
Madan Lal	12	2	31	3
Binny	10	1	23	1
Amarnath	7	0	12	3
Azad	3	0	7	0

Mohinder Amarnath, the man of the match in the 1983 World Cup final. A fluent player in normal circumstances, Amarnath struggled to 26 from 80 balls, which should have alerted the West Indies batsmen to the difficult nature of the Lord's pitch.
(Getty Images/Touchline Photo)

Ravi Shastri was India's twelfth man in the match. He said: 'I was sitting in the dressing room when the guys came off the park and I don't think any of us thought it was enough, but we realised it was a knockout game and that we had nothing to lose. There was only one team that could lose it from that point and that was the West Indies and that's exactly what happened.

'The moment we realised we had a chance was when Viv got out. Viv was the best batsman in the world and the way he started off was as if he had a plane to catch. He smashed 33 off 28 balls and it took a great running catch by Kapil Dev to get rid of him. He made it look easy, but it was an outstanding catch under pressure because he had to run all the way from short midwicket to about 10 yards from the boundary line.

'And then when Clive Lloyd got out caught in the covers I can remember clearly the dressing room erupted, even though there were only five or six of us in it! We thought at 66 for five that here is a definite chance and you knew that there was a match on.'

As it turned out, India's medium pacers were ideally suited to the pitch. Balwinder Singh Sandhu made the new ball swing all over the place and in mid-innings Amarnath proved virtually impossible to get away. Shastri said: 'Sandu was military medium, but he was deadly accurate and a clever bowler who swung it both ways and enjoyed bowling in English conditions. He played all his cricket for Bombay and he always came across to me as a cricketer who played above his potential: a limited player, but one who knew his limitations.

'Mohinder Amarnath was an example of someone who in those conditions could roll his arm over for seven or eight overs and give nothing away and of course he got three wickets. He was accurate and he bowled to his field and when he got Jeff Dujon to play on playing no shot he couldn't believe it; he was livid.'

In the foreground, the World Cup. Behind, the two men who did most to win it for India, Kapil Dev (left) and Mohinder Amarnath.
(Getty Images/Touchline Photo)

Dujon was a flamboyant player who had reined himself in to rebuild the innings from the tatters of 76 for six. He had grafted his way to 25 from 73 balls when he was a little late in lifting the bat to a ball outside off stump. The ball hit the back of the bat and cannoned on to the stumps. From 119 for seven there was no way back and Holding was the last man out, lbw to Amarnath who finished with the incredible figures of 7-0-12-3.

According to Holding: 'I came in as last man when we batted and I was almost in shock because I didn't expect us to be in that position. You always try to be positive, but with Garner and myself at the wicket and 50 runs to get, realistically we were out of it.

'As a match it was a complete one off. We played India in the Caribbean shortly afterwards, won four of the six Tests and every one-day game. Having said that, though, India beat us in the preliminary round of the World Cup at Old Trafford as well as in the final, so they might say that they had our number at that time.'

That was certainly Shastri's opinion. I asked him whether India had in fact arrived at the right pitch in the right place at the right time for the attack they had and he said, 'Yes, absolutely. In fact, right tournament. It was the time of the year where the conditions were such that it suited the Indian attack. But India played as a team right through the tournament and there was a great camaraderie. We beat all the top teams: the West Indies twice, England and Australia and for a season or so either side of the World Cup we were a very good side.'

The result ignited passion for the one-day game in India and to this day 183 is regarded as the magic number by the team and their supporters. Whatever the conditions, if India scores 183 or more they always believe they can win the game.

Facing page: *Ravi Shastri.*
(Getty Images/Touchline Photo)

Sensation in Sharjah

Two years after their World Cup triumph, India played the World Series triangular tournament in Australia and ended up beating Pakistan in the final. A week after that they played in Sharjah in what Ravi Shastri called 'the greatest one-day game I have played in or watched in my life'.

'We won our two preliminary games,' he said, 'and again played Pakistan in the final. We batted first and were shot out for 125 by Imran Khan who bowled an outstanding spell and took six for 14. We sat in the dressing room between innings and the amazing thing was that very few people thought we would lose! That's how confident we were as a side around that time. Pakistan reached 40 for two and then a run-out took place. Next thing you knew they were 87 all out and we'd won comfortably.

'It was a seriously good Pakistan side, but the game was turned on its head. They just panicked. I got Javed Miandad in my first over and then the leg-spinner Sivaramakrishnan at the other end got Ashraf Ali and Imran and suddenly from 40 for two they were 60 for five and that's when they lost the plot.'

Salim Malik dug in, but towards the end of his spell Shastri had him caught at slip by Gavaskar and when Kapil Dev came back into the attack the last four wickets fell for two runs and India had won by the relatively substantial margin of 38 runs.

Rothmans Four-Nations Cup
India v Pakistan
Sharjah C.A. Stadium
22 March 1985 (50-overs match)

Result: India won by 38 runs

India innings
RJ Shastri lbw *b* Imran Khan 0
K Srikkanth *c* Saleem Malik *b* Imran Khan 6
M Azharuddin *b* Tauseef Ahmed 47
DB Vengsarkar *c* Ashraf Ali *b* Imran Khan 1
SM Gavaskar *c* Ashraf Ali *b* Imran Khan 2
M Amarnath *b* Imran Khan 5
*N Kapil Dev *b* Tauseef Ahmed 30
RMH Binny *c* Javed Miandad *b* Mudassar Nazar ...8
S Madan Lal *c* Ashraf Ali *b* Imran Khan 11
+S Viswanath not out 3
L Sivaramakrishnan *c* Salim Malik *b* Wasim Akram..1
Extras (b 5, lb 4, w 2) 11
Total (all out, 42.4 overs) 125

FoW: 1-0 (Shastri), 2-12 (Srikkanth), 3-20 (Vengsarkar), 4-28 (Gavaskar), 5-34 (Amarnath), 6-80 (Kapil Dev), 7-95 (Binny), 8-113 (Madan Lal), 9-121 (Azharuddin), 10-125 (Sivaramakrishnan).

Bowling	O	M	R	W
Imran Khan	10	2	14	6
Wasim Akram	7.4	0	27	1
Tahir Naqqash	5	0	12	0
Mudassar Nazar	10	1	36	1
Tauseef Ahmed	10	0	27	2

Pakistan innings
Mudassar Nazar *c* Gavaskar *b* Binny 18
Mohsin Khan run out 10
Rameez Raja *c* Gavaskar *b* Kapil Dev 29
*Javed Miandad *c* Gavaskar *b* Shastri 0
+Ashraf Ali *c* Vengsarkar *b* Siva'krishnan 0
Imran Khan st Viswanath *b* Siva'krishnan 0
Salim Malik *c* Gavaskar *b* Shastri 17
Manzoor Elahi *c & b* Madan Lal 9
Tahir Naqqash *c* Viswanath *b* Kapil Dev 1
Tauseef Ahmed *b* Kapil Dev 0
Wasim Akram not out 0
Extras (lb 1, w 1, nb 1) 3
Total (all out, 32.5 overs) 87

FoW: 1-13 (Mohsin Khan), 2-35 (Mudassar Nazar), 3-40 (Javed Miandad), 4-41 (Ashraf Ali), 5-41 (Imran Khan), 6-74 (Salim Malik), 7-85 (Rameez Raja), 8-87 (Tahir Naqqash), 9-87 (Manzoor Elahi), 10-87 (Tauseef Ahmed).

Bowling	O	M	R	W
Kapil Dev	6.5	1	17	3
Binny	3	0	24	1
Siva'krishnan	7	2	16	2
Shastri	10	5	17	2
Madan Lal	6	2	12	1

Sachin Tendulkar

I'm reminded of something written seventy years ago by Raymond Robertson-Glasgow. He wrote of the great Kent and England left-hander: 'Frank Woolley was easy to watch, difficult to bowl to and impossible to write about. When you bowled to him there weren't enough fielders; when you wrote about him there weren't enough words. In describing a great innings by Woolley, and few of them were not great in artistry, you had to go careful with your adjectives and stack them in little rows, like pats of butter or razor-blades.

'In the first over of his innings, perhaps, there had been an exquisite off-drive, followed by a perfect cut, then an effortless leg-glide. In the second over the same sort of thing happened; and your superlatives had already gone. The best thing to do was presume that your readers knew how Frank Woolley batted and use no adjectives at all.'

That's pretty much how I feel about Sachin Tendulkar, but I can't express it as well as 'Crusoe'. When Tendulkar first played for India he was still at school and didn't own a razor. In 1990 he came to England for the first time; India lost the first Test and were 109 for four on the final day of the second at Old Trafford when Tendulkar came to the crease. Four hours later he was still batting, having scored his first Test century, 119 not out, and the match was saved. He was sixteen.

This chapter should be filled with scorecards extolling the genius of Tendulkar, the most complete batsman since Bradman, a master of both Test and one-day cricket. It is not, because how do you decide on one or two innings? Even Ravi Shastri was at a loss and instead of singling out one knock he said: 'Tendulkar's batting in the series against Australia in India in 1997 was something else. He was in prime form and whether it was pace or spin the ball just kept disappearing to the boundary.'

Note that Shastri, too, doesn't waste adjectives but assumes that people know how Tendulkar bats. Opponents know that they have to get him quickly or there's a chance they won't get him at all. The crowd know they had better be in their seats early. He is on the stage so often that we have become blasé about Tendulkar, but one day he'll be gone and those of us lucky enough to have watched him will bore our grandchildren talking about him. 'Yes,' we'll say, 'your fellow X is a good player, but you should have seen Tendulkar.'

Three studies in mastery. Sachin Tendulkar has scored more one-day centuries than any player in history and if he stays fit he will inevitably break every batting record in the game. The secret to his batting is that there is no secret: bowl it short and he'll cut you to ribbons (above), *over-pitch and he'll hit you straight* (bottom left), *give him width and he'll make cover's life a misery* (top left).

When he first played for India he wore a pair of Sunil Gavaskar's old pads, a sign that India's greatest player knew that a better one had come along. Ravi Shastri recalls: 'The '83 World Cup ignited a passion for the one-day game in India. After that it was a totally different scenario. The interest and enthusiasm for the game in the streets was amazing. In that five-year period we won a lot of tournaments and when you win it has an impact. You could argue that Tendulkar came out of that period with people wanting to emulate the established players.'
(Getty Images/Touchline Photo)

The greatest leg spinner the game has ever seen, Australia's Shane Warne. (Getty Images/Touchline Photo)

While one-day cricket began in England, which was also the venue of the first three World Cups, it's fair to say that the catalyst for most of the important developments, certainly in ODI cricket, has been Australia. However, the Australian Cricket Board (ACB) was every bit as conservative as its counterpart in England up until the point when one man held a gun to its head.

If ever a man went from arch villain to knight in shining armour it was Kerry Packer. In 1977 Packer was reputed to be Australia's wealthiest man and among other enterprises he ran the independent Australian television company, Channel Nine. In a bid to challenge the state-owned television networks, he decided to bid for the rights to show Test cricket and upon that whim professional cricket changed for ever.

Packer put in a bid for the exclusive rights to top cricket in Australia and although he offered far more than the Australian Broadcasting Commission (ABC), the ACB accepted ABC's offer without listening to Packer's proposals. It was a high-handed decision that insulted Packer and he set out to make the ACB pay for its arrogance.

In 1976 Packer and his agents set about contracting major Test cricketers with the intention of staging international matches independent of both the ACB and ABC. Twenty-eight top Australians signed together with forty others, largely from the West Indies and England. Amongst them was the current England captain, the South African-born Tony Greig.

Rumours of the impending drama surfaced at the Centenary Test match between Australia and England at the Melbourne Cricket Ground (MCG) in March 1977 and by the time Australia arrived in England for the Ashes tour two months later, all hell had broken loose.

The England selectors were instructed by the Test and County Cricket Board (TCCB) not to select Greig as captain and there were also threats of Test match bans for players who had signed with Packer. It was the same knee-jerk reaction that Channel Nine had been given by the ACB and both they and the TCCB had naively assumed that the players would buckle under their threats.

They reckoned without Packer's determination and he travelled to England to open discussions with the authorities. The talks broke down when the ACB refused to agree to Packer's demand for exclusive television rights as soon as the existing ABC contract ended.

The ICC divided the cricket world into two camps when it issued a proclamation that said, 'No player who, after October 1st 1977 has played or has made himself available to play in a match previously disapproved by the conference shall thereafter be eligible to play in any Test match.'

Kerry Packer, reputed to be Australia's wealthiest man at the time, on his way from court in England in 1977. The confident smile suggests that he knows he's on the winning side.
(Getty Images/Touchline Photo)

'You'll forgive me if I give a lot of credit for the healthy financial position of Australian cricket to one man who is criticised frequently, Kerry Packer . . . I thank him for what he did because I think that was the catalyst that brought cricket to where it is today.' – ACB representative Bob Parish upon his retirement in 1992.
(Getty Images/Touchline Photo)

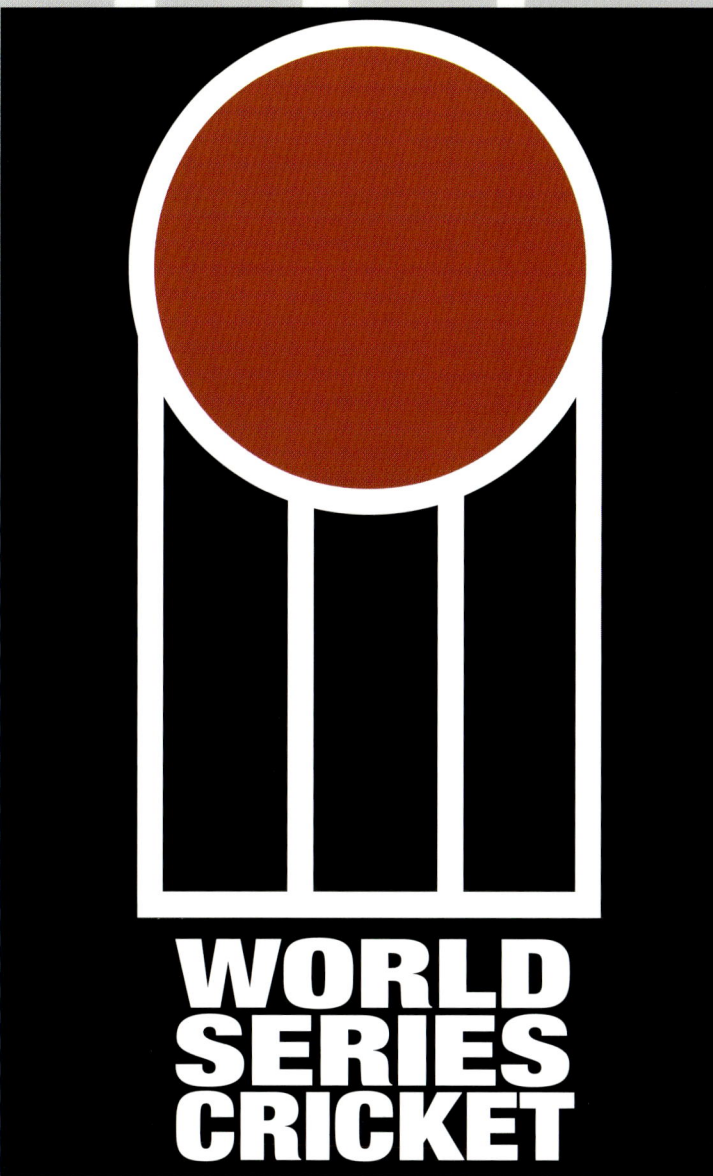

Kerry Packer's World Series Cricket logo. Before the first WSC game Packer's marketing men had rolled out merchandise speckled with this logo. It was another example of his organisation being ahead of the game; branding is seen as a basic requirement today, but in 1978 nobody in cricket deemed it important.
(Getty Images/Touchline Photo)

Packer, Greig, John Snow and South African allrounder Mike Procter took the ICC and the TCCB to court and won costs estimated at £250 000. To put that figure in perspective, it was two and a half times as much as the sponsorship of the 1975 World Cup. Mr Justice Slade saw the ban as being an unreasonable restraint of trade.

That did not stop the TCCB and ACB banning players who had signed contracts with Packer, however, and for the next three years international cricket bore a watered-down look as teams took the field woefully short of full strength. The harsh reality was that Packer had identified a major financial anomaly in the game and simply exploited the fact that Test cricketers, other than those playing in English county cricket, were still poorly paid in the 1970s.

To underline Packer's acuity, Cornhill Insurance became the first major sponsor of the England cricket team in 1978, putting up £1 million in a five-year deal. England players received £1 000 each for playing a Test and that winter the fee for touring New Zealand and Pakistan increased from £3 000 to £5 000. It was still not a king's ransom, but in comparison to what had been on offer prior to Packer's intervention it was at least a decent living. The irony of the situation, however, was that while Packer wanted a bigger and better form of Test cricket for Channel Nine, what he actually created was a hothouse atmosphere for the development of the one-day game.

Even in an environment such as Packer's there was a reverence for Test cricket that precluded real innovation and, ultimately, real involvement for either the crowd or the players. World Series Cricket (WSC), as it was known, ran for three years and featured several outstanding individual feats, but they were largely irrelevant because the players and the crowd knew that this was not 'proper' Test cricket. By contrast, ODI cricket was still youthful enough to have no emotional baggage to drag along with it and it was here that WSC earned its place in history.

Coloured clothing, floodlights, black sightscreens, white balls and fielding circles came together for the first time in WSC. Because Packer's games were banned from most first class cricket grounds, they were played at venues more normally associated with Aussie Rules Football, grounds which tended to have floodlights. So while cricket pitches grown in greenhouses and deposited in the middle of football fields may have appeared as strange bedfellows, the juxtaposition of cricket and floodlights turned out to be a marriage made in heaven.

Three teams played the first season of WSC – Australia, West Indies and the Rest of the World. Channel Nine's 315 hours of TV coverage attracted reasonable audiences not least because of the innovative way in which the matches were televised, the techniques being a vast improvement on the staid methods of the BBC and ABC.

And in addition to the television audience, night cricket was a hit with the paying spectators almost from day one. In January 1978 two night games were held at VFL Park in Melbourne attracting crowds of 17 000 and 24 000, a huge improvement on the 2 500 average daily attendance at Packer's five-day Super Tests. The knock-on effect of having good crowds at the grounds was greater entertainment value for the television audience.

Viewers of those early night games all made the point that the coloured clothing and white ball enhanced the cricket, even if the floodlights made it seem slightly unreal. There was also the unusual sight in 1978 of players wearing crash helmets. Greig and Barry Richards, the great South African opening batsman, wore white motorcycle helmets that were a far cry from the ones in use in the game today.

These protective measures were due to a suspicion that the hothouse pitches were not quite what they had been cracked up to be, but they seemed to spur opposition fast bowlers to bowl even more bouncers, something they could do with impunity as there were no restrictions on short-pitched bowling.

But just when it seemed as though WSC was here to stay, in May 1979 the ACB came to an agreement with Packer, conceding to all his demands, and seemingly more, in a ten-year deal worth A$1,15 million per year. The scheduled Test series between Australia and India was cancelled, and replaced by the 15-match Benson and Hedges World Series Cup, a triangular series with the West Indies and England. Crucially, the ACB agreed to use one of the staples of WSC, coloured clothing.

One of the ACB representatives during the three years of Packer-induced turmoil was Bob Parish. When Parish retired in 1992 he had this to say: 'You'll forgive me if I give a lot of credit for the healthy financial position of Australian cricket to one man who is criticised frequently, Kerry Packer . . . I thank him for what he did because I think that was the catalyst that brought cricket to where it is today.'

A quarter of a century later Packer still controls the broadcasting of cricket in Australia and, among other things, is directly responsible for the shamelessly chauvinistic commentary that emanates from there. Packer will not tolerate those who are not one hundred per cent behind the product and sacked Rodney Marsh from the commentary team when the former Test wicketkeeper dared to suggest that one-day cricket was irrelevant and that Test matches were what really mattered.

He has, however, earned a reputation for being fiercely loyal and when Tony Greig could no longer earn a living as a cricketer in England, Packer created the commentary job that Greig still relishes to this day. Early in the year 2002 Packer sent out first class plane tickets to the class of '77, who were flown to Sydney for a twenty-fifth birthday party of conspicuous hedonism. Packer can do all this because he is still immensely rich and, more importantly, he was right. He was right to believe that the public wanted above all else to be entertained and the strength of Australian cricket today has much to do with the complete overhaul given to it during, and in the wake of, WSC.

One of the things that makes the current Australian team so dominant is the pace at which they score their runs. That is the direct result of a marketing decision taken soon after WSC. One-day cricket had proved that the public wanted action, it therefore seemed logical that if five an over was easily achievable in the shortened form of the game, it should be equally possible in Test matches where there were, perforce, fewer boundary fielders. When Adam Gilchrist scored a double century against South Africa at the Wanderers in February 2002 he scored it at a run a ball. That is not supposed to happen in a Test match. It is a direct result of the influence of one-day cricket.

Two sides of South African cricket come together in one of Kerry Packer's Super-Tests. Barry Richards is the man under the helmet, the best opening batsman in world cricket in the 1970s who, due to South Africa's sporting isolation, played only four Test matches. Richards is wearing one of the first batting helmets as protection against short-pitched bowling, upon which there was no restriction in WSC, and against the poor wickets that hothouse procedures sometimes produced.

Kepler Wessels, the fielder in this picture, played county cricket in England for Sussex and then went to Australia where he earned a residential qualification to play for the national team. Wessels made a century against England on Test debut and had a successful career in both Test and ODI cricket for his adopted country, but some fourteen years after this picture was taken he led an official South African team on to the field at the 1992 World Cup.
(Getty Images/Touchline Photo)

Glory for Gilchrist

South Africa and Australia had been playing each other for the best part of six months when they met for the fifth ODI of a seven-match series at St George's Park in Port Elizabeth. During that time Australia had proved beyond question that they were the best team in the world and that, furthermore, there was a huge gap in ability between them and everyone else. They won the Test series 5-1 (three Tests in Australia, three in South Africa) and the win at Port Elizabeth gave them a 5-0 lead in the ODI series. They were being talked about as the best Australian side ever, an accolade usually accorded Don Bradman's 1948 Ashes winners.

What set this team apart was its astonishing confidence. On the rare occasions when wickets fell early there was no let up in the stroke play and in the Test matches the real fun only started when the fifth wicket fell. That was the cue for Adam Gilchrist to emerge from the pavilion and pulverise the bowling.

Gilchrist's representative career began late, due to the long-term presence in the team of wicketkeeper Ian Healy. His chance came in ODIs before Tests and he was used as an opening batsman. He was given licence to play like Sanath Jayasuriya did for Sri Lanka and he rarely disappointed. But it was only when Healy retired that Gilchrist's career went into overdrive. First his wicketkeeping improved and with it his confidence. By the time he came to South Africa he was the complete package and in all forms of the game he batted as if the bowlers were delivering footballs.

The astonishing aspect of Gilchrist's tour was that he never needed time to play himself in. Everything came out of the middle of the bat and South Africa's captains, Mark Boucher and Shaun Pollock, soon gave up any pretence of trying to dismiss him, they just hoped he would hit one to a boundary fielder and be forced to take a single. At St George's Park South Africa were on a hiding to nothing. They had made 326 for three in 50 overs, a great score based upon wonderful hitting from Jacques Kallis and Jonty Rhodes. But Australia had wrapped the series up in the previous match and with nothing to lose set out on an apparently impossible task.

The 50 came up in the fifth over, the 100 in the twelfth. Gilchrist reached 50 off 27 balls, was bowled by a no-ball and then legitimately dismissed for 52, and even then it took an incredible boundary catch by Makhaya Ntini to get rid of him. In mid-innings Australia's new captain Ricky Ponting and Darren Lehmann took control so impressively that the result was virtually assured by the 25th over. Ponting made 92, Lehmann 91, but when the man of the match award was given to Gilchrist there was not a dissenting voice.

In South Africa in 2002 Adam Gilchrist entered a vein of form so rich that no one could bowl to him. He entered the fray at number seven in the Test series, but in the ODIs he opened, which meant that the crowd were always in their seats early.
(Getty Images/Touchline Photo)

In the series against South Africa in 2002 Adam Gilchrist scored the fastest Test double century of all time. All he did was play as though it was an ODI, the culmination of fifteen years' planning by the ACB and the Australian Academy.
(Getty Images/Touchline Photo)

South Africa v Australia
St George's Park, Port Elizabeth
6 April 2002 (50-over match)

Result: Australia won by 3 wickets

South Africa innings
GC Smith *c* Lehmann *b* Warne	84
HH Gibbs *c* & *b* Harvey	37
N Boje *b* Lehmann	47
JH Kallis not out	80
JN Rhodes not out	71
Extras (lb 5, w 2)	7
Total (3 wickets, 50 overs)	**326**

DNB: ND McKenzie, +MV Boucher, *SM Pollock, JC Kent, M Ntini, R Telemachus.

FoW: 1-74 (Gibbs), 2-157 (Boje), 3-194 (Smith).

Bowling	O	M	R	W
McGrath	10	2	52	0
Gillespie	9	0	60	0
Harvey	9	0	64	1
Warne	7	0	58	1
Watson	9	0	47	0
Lehmann	6	0	40	1

Australia innings
+AC Gilchrist *c* Ntini *b* Telemachus	52
ML Hayden *c* Pollock *b* Kallis	35
IJ Harvey *c* Boucher *b* Telemachus	4
*RT Ponting *c* Pollock *b* Kallis	92
DS Lehmann *st* Boucher *b* Smith	91
DR Martyn *c* Rhodes *b* Ntini	15
MG Bevan not out	3
SR Watson run out (Boje)	11
SK Warne not out	4
Extras (b 2, lb 7, w 6, nb 8)	23
Total (7 wickets, 49.1 overs)	**330**

DNB: JN Gillespie, GD McGrath.

FoW: 1-81 (Gilchrist), 2-93 (Harvey), 3-104 (Hayden), 4-287 (Lehmann), 5-312 (Martyn), 6-312 (Ponting), 7-326 (Watson).

Bowling	O	M	R	W
Pollock	8	0	57	0
Ntini	9.1	0	83	1
Telemachus	10	0	48	2
Kallis	10	0	59	2
Boje	6	0	34	0
Kent	2	0	16	0
Smith	4	0	24	1

Michael Bevan

In the mid-1970s it was suggested that one-day cricket was detrimental to the development of Test players. English county cricket in particular seemed to be top heavy with 'bits and pieces players', people who could bat a bit and bowl a bit, few of whom would ever make it into a first class side on the merits of one discipline. But as one-day cricket developed into a money-spinning form of the game, selectors realised that there was a place for the specialist, a player who might have too many technical flaws for the Test arena, but who could change the course of a one-day game in half an hour of inspired batting or bowling.

The best example of a specialist the game has yet provided is Michael Bevan. The Australian left-hander looked set for a long and successful Test career, but continued exposure to the highest form of the game revealed a fatal flaw against fast, short-pitched bowling. One-day cricket by its very nature does not allow that kind of bowling for very long and so Bevan was able to prosper. He established a reputation early on as a great organiser of the final overs, be they to set a target or to overhaul one, and today he is regarded as the nonpareil, the perfect one-day batsman.

Which is not to say that Bevan is a destroyer of bowling like Lance Klusener, or that he plays shots impossible for anyone else like Sachin Tendulkar. What Bevan does is to make a mockery of nervous tension. He exemplifies the truism among professional cricketers that there is always more time than you think. This game against New Zealand is perhaps the best example of all in a career that has made a mockery of the accepted facts of ODI cricket. He scored 102 not out from 95 balls, but hit only seven fours. He did it with just the tail for company and without for one moment suggesting that run scoring was difficult.

New Zealand needed only to win to reach the final of the VB series and they had virtually won the game by the time Bevan came in. Stephen Fleming won the toss and chose to bat; 245 for eight was the more than satisfactory result. Then the bowlers went to work and with a little help in the pitch and through the air for the pacemen, Shane Bond, Dion Nash and Andre Adams reduced Australia to 82 for six halfway through the 22nd over.

Bevan had come in at 53 for four and had scarcely put bat to ball when Shane Warne emerged from the pavilion, more in hope than expectation. But one of the basic tenets of Bevan's one-day philosophy is that there is no such thing as a lost cause. He set about repairing the damage in such matter of fact fashion that the opposition remained absurdly confident of victory. New Zealand were in such command that even a stand of 61 between Bevan and

Left: *Michael Bevan reaches three figures in the penultimate over against New Zealand at the MCG. He scored 102 not out from 95 balls, but only hit seven fours in an innings devoid of risk, played with Australian backs to the wall throughout. The bemused expression on the face of wicketkeeper Adam Parore says it all: you can't play against that.*
(Getty Images/Touchline Photo)

VB Series, 2001/02
Australia v New Zealand
Melbourne Cricket Ground (day/night)
29 January 2002 (50-over match)

Result: Australia won by 2 wickets

New Zealand innings
L Vincent c Gilchrist b McGrath 5
NJ Astle c Warne b Lee 11
*SP Fleming run out (SR Waugh/Warne) ...50
CD McMillan c Ponting b Harvey 34
CL Cairns c Bevan b Warne 55
CZ Harris run out (Warne/Harvey) 41
DJ Nash run out (Harvey) 24
+AC Parore lbw b McGrath 1
AR Adams not out 13
DL Vettori not out 0
Extras (lb 4, w 4, nb 3) 11
Total (8 wickets, 50 overs, 206 mins) 245

DNB: SE Bond.

FoW: 1-7 (Vincent), 2-19 (Astle), 3-73 (McMillan), 4-143 (Fleming), 5-178 (Cairns), 6-226 (Nash), 7-228 (Parore), 8-235 (Harris).

Bowling	O	M	R	W
McGrath	10	0	41	2
Lee	8	0	32	1
Bichel	6	0	20	0
Warne	10	0	56	1
Harvey	10	0	59	1
SR Waugh	6	0	33	0

Australia innings
ME Waugh c Adams b Nash 21
+AC Gilchrist b Bond 14
RT Ponting c Astle b Bond 8
DR Martyn c Harris b Adams 6
*SR Waugh c Parore b Nash 7
MG Bevan not out 102
IJ Harvey c Parore b Bond 12
SK Warne c Bond b Adams 29
B Lee c Astle b Bond 27
AJ Bichel not out 13
Extras (w 3, nb 6) 9
Total (8 wickets, 49.3 overs) 248

DNB: GD McGrath.

FoW: 1-24 (Gilchrist), 2-40 (Ponting), 3-51 (ME Waugh), 4-53 (Martyn), 5-65 (SR Waugh), 6-82 (Harvey), 7-143 (Warne), 8-224 (Lee).

Bowling	O	M	R	W
Nash	9	0	50	2
Bond	9.3	2	38	4
Adams	10	0	52	2
Vettori	10	0	36	0
Harris	8	0	50	0
Astle	3	0	22	0

Steve Waugh hoists the trophy after winning the 1999 World Cup. Australia beat Pakistan in comprehensive fashion by eight wickets.
(Getty Images/Touchline Photo)

Warne mattered little, for when Warne was caught in the deep for 29 there were still 103 runs required from 80 balls with three wickets in hand.

The next partnership changed the course of the match. Bevan began to manipulate the strike, and suddenly New Zealand, not Australia, were chasing the game. One of the secrets of Bevan's batting is that his mastery gives confidence to his partner and while he dominated the strike, Lee, when he did get away from the bowler's end, was able to play without shackles. He hit 27 from 29 balls in a stand worth 81 and by the time he was out 22 were needed from 15 balls.

In came Andy Bichel, a man with a first class century to his name, but no great pedigree in ODIs. Now, almost for the first time, Bevan became utterly dominant. Rather than lashing out in risky attempts to hit boundaries he utilised the enormous playing surface of the MCG and, placing the ball with surgical precision, coaxed his partner into running twos. He reached his hundred in the penultimate over and when the last one began with Bichel on strike a further five were required. Bichel hit two out of three deliveries to the point boundary and Australia had won by two wickets with three balls to spare.

The end was fitting, for Bevan has only rarely needed to thrash the last ball to the boundary in a run chase; usually, as was the case here, he has such control that such pyrotechnics would seem almost vulgar. You sense that he would far rather leave the limelight to the man at the other end and plod back to the pavilion for a cold beer, with yet another not out against his name. And that is the final secret of Bevan's game: he is incredibly difficult to get out. He might not score as many runs as the great Tendulkar, but while the Little Master averages 44, Bevan averages 57.

South Africa

During two decades of isolation, cricket in South Africa did not stand still. With no one else to play against, the South African administrators became quite bold and were happy to try out new ideas, particularly in one-day cricket. The fielding circle was first used in South Africa, the initial premise being nine players inside the circle for the first 10 overs, then six for the rest of the innings. The South Africans who played World Series Cricket took this idea with them and, in an example of cross pollination, brought back with them the news that night cricket was the future of the game at one-day level.

In an attempt to keep Test cricket alive in the country, the administrators organised a number of so-called 'Rebel Tours' during the 1980s, the principal effect of which was to harden other countries' stance against South Africa. The last of the tours was by an England team led by Mike Gatting in 1989/90 and it caused so much acrimony that it was abandoned halfway through. It continued long enough, however, for one remarkable innings to be played.

The mighty Adrian Kuiper showing a deft touch as he glances to leg. Kuiper scored a century off 49 balls against Mike Gatting's rebel England team at Bloemfontein in 1990.
(Touchline Photo)

Adrian Kuiper's Century in Bloemfontein

Adrian Kuiper was (and is) an apple farmer in the Cape with forearms like a grown man's thigh. He began his cricket career as a genuine allrounder, but a shoulder operation stifled his quick bowling ambitions and forced him to concentrate more on his destructive batting. Kuiper was one of the unfortunates who lost the best part of his career to isolation, and although he was a member of the first South African teams to play after readmission, he was never able to reproduce the form he showed against Gatting's rebels.

Kuiper remembers the day well. 'I was having one of those seasons, which was quite strange because in December I was laid up in hospital with meningitis! I was in hospital for a week and then went home to rest for another week and I was having incredible headaches, but from the moment I started playing again I just started performing. I scored runs in every game in which I played and I was very confident every time I went to the wicket.

'I had been scoring runs before I went to hospital as well and I remember getting a hundred in a benefit game in Pretoria where I hit Corrie van Zyl and Allan Donald around a bit. I was twenty-nine going on thirty and at the peak of my career. I didn't score many hundreds because I tended to bat at number five or lower, but that season I batted a lot at number four.

'In the match against England at Springbok Park we won the toss and batted first on a very good pitch. Jimmy Cook and Henry Fotheringham opened the batting for us. Peter Kirsten was due in at number three and I was irritating him a little bit while he was waiting to bat, saying, "Why don't these guys get on with it, that should be going over midwicket", stuff like that. In the end he told me to buzz off and sit somewhere else.

'But that was the kind of positive frame of mind I was in, even though England had a good attack. Greg Thomas, Richard Ellison and Paul Jarvis were the seamers and John Emburey the spinner. I eventually got to the wicket with the score on 128 for two and Thomas bowled me a short delivery. I mishit it and it just spooned over mid-on for two.

'The next over I got the strike and I was facing Ellison who bowled very nice away-swingers. He bowled me a ball that pitched on leg stump. I put my foot down and hit it out of the ground and into the rugby stadium. And then it just started.

'The next over I hit Thomas over cover for six, then pulled him over midwicket for another and it was just uncanny because my timing was absolutely perfect. John Emburey came on and I went down the pitch to his first ball and hit him straight. Now, Springbok Park is a big ground, but it cleared the grass bank at the Loch Logan End by 10 metres.

---

20 February 1990
Springbok Park, Bloemfontein
55 overs per side

Result: South Africa won by 207 runs

South Africa innings:
*SJ Cook c French b Ellison 73
HR Fotheringham c and b Gatting 17
PN Kirsten b Gatting 40
AP Kuiper b Jarvis 117
CEB Rice b Gatting 0
+TR Madsen c Broad b Barnett 18
DJ Cullinan run out 12
MW Rushmere not out 11
TG Shaw not out 1
Extras (lb 2, w 10) 12
Total (7 wickets, 50 overs) 301

DNB: PS de Villiers, AA Donald

FoW: 1-33 (Fotheringham), 2-128 (Cook), 3-204 (Kirsten), 4-204 (Rice), 5-277 (Kuiper), 6-277 (Madsen), 7-300 (Cullinan)

Bowling:	O	M	R	W
Jarvis	10	1	38	1
Thomas	8	2	33	0
Gatting	9	1	54	3
Ellison	8	0	48	1
Emburey	10	0	57	0
Cowdrey	4	0	23	0
Barnett	6	0	46	1

English XI
BC Broad b de Villiers 1
KJ Barnett b Donald 1
CWJ Athey c Madsen b Rice 50
*MW Gatting b Donald 3
MP Maynard b Donald 0
CS Cowdrey c Fotheringham b Rice 4
JE Emburey b Shaw 2
JG Thomas c and b Shaw 2
+BN French c Madsen b Kuiper 4
PW Jarvis lbw b Kuiper 1
RM Ellison not out 7
Extras (b 6, lb 6, w 5, nb 1) 18
Total (all out, 45.1 overs) 94

FoW: 1-2 (Barnett), 2-8 (Broad), 3-16 (Gatting), 4-23 (Maynard), 5-30 (Cowdrey), 6-37 (Emburey), 7-39 (Thomas), 8-57 (French), 9-63 (Jarvis), 10-94 (Athey)

Bowling:	O	M	R	W
Donald	8	2	11	3
De Villiers	8	2	16	1
Rice	7.1	1	11	2
Shaw	11	4	15	2
Kuiper	8	0	24	2
Kirsten	3	1	3	0

'Mike Gatting came on and I got hold of him a bit and I ended up scoring a hundred off 49 balls, but the statistic I remember is that when I got to 50 Peter Kirsten had scored two! He never got the strike and had to be content to stand at the other end and watch. The funny thing was that the first 50 was quicker than the second one because that's when I hit most of my sixes.'

Kuiper's century came off 49 balls with eight sixes and seven fours. His last 17 runs came at the relatively sedate pace of a run a ball and after passing three figures he only hit one more boundary (a four) and was dropped on 109. Among the spectators was a young Hansie Cronjé, who could not have dreamt at that moment that he would one day play in an official South African team that included Kuiper.

Said Cronjé: 'I was playing for Free State and the players were given great seats to watch the game. The ground was just one year old and the pitch never bounced above knee height, which made it very difficult to get the ball away, but that didn't seem to worry Adrian! I remember a shot off Greg Thomas, which went over square leg into the tennis courts, another one over mid-off, also off Thomas, and he got stuck into Mike Gatting and hit him into the Zoo.

'The funny part about the game was that after SA made over 300, Gatting's team came in to bat and the lights went out! But the umpires said the game had to go on and they had to face Donald at his quickest, Fanie de Villiers and a few others with the lights not working!'

In fact only one of the four floodlight stanchions lost power, but not surprisingly it was a one-sided contest and Gatting's team were dismissed for just 94 runs. Four years later, after a spell out of the team, Kuiper was recalled for the one-day series against Australia. Cronjé said: 'The golden moment came at the end of our innings at Centurion in the second ODI, when Adrian hit Craig McDermott for three successive sixes off the last three balls of the innings. He got 47 off 22 balls and we ended up winning the game comfortably because of that innings.'

Late in 1991 South Africa was readmitted to international competition. The cricketers went on a three-match ODI tour to India and in February 1992 Kuiper and Cronjé were both part of the fifteen-man squad that went to the fifth World Cup in Australia and New Zealand.

The Catch That Never Was

South Africa began their first World Cup in a most emphatic manner, with a nine-wicket win against the reigning world champions in Sydney. But as much as the ease with which Kepler Wessels and Peter Kirsten stroked them to victory, the abiding memory of the game is of the catch that never was.

Australia won the toss and chose to bat, Allan Donald bowled the first ball to Geoff Marsh, who nicked it to wicketkeeper Dave Richardson, stood his ground and was given not out by New Zealand umpire Brian Aldridge. For the huge television audience watching around the world it seemed an immense injustice. Replays showed how clear the deflection had been: Richardson took it in front of first slip. Many batsmen would have walked, but not Marsh. Hansie Cronjé takes up the story.

'It was my first international and also for Mark Rushmere, Jonty Rhodes and a few others. It was like this golden moment as we came back into international cricket and the build-up to the first ball seemed to take about twenty minutes. Allan bowled and we knew that Geoff Marsh had nicked it, but we were so surprised and I think the umpire was too. I was standing at third man and I could hear it.

'Later I got to know him (Aldridge) quite well and he said to me that Allan was simply too quick! He was looking down for a no ball and when he looked up the ball was already in Dave Richardson's gloves. He saw it a few times afterwards on television and realised that he had made the wrong decision.

A stunning view of the Sydney Cricket ground as night falls. Kepler Wessels is about to face the first ball of the innings from Bruce Reid, Andrew Hudson is at the non-striker's end. Brian Aldridge, the New Zealand umpire who denied Allan Donald the wicket of Geoff Marsh with the first ball of the match is adjusting his hat at square leg. Despite Aldridge's error, South Africa won their first World Cup match by the emphatic margin of nine wickets.
(Getty Images/Touchline Photo)

'I think he was right about Allan being too quick. If you look at his action through his career it was probably at its best around 1992/93 because he swung the ball away from the right-handers. In that tournament we used two white balls, one from each end, and Dave Richardson stood a long way back.

'Because we were new at that level we didn't make a big thing about it. Everyone knew it was out and we trotted up to congratulate the bowler. If the same thing had happened a few years later you would have seen the wicketkeeper catch the ball, run a few yards and throw it in the air. If you do that the umpire is usually convinced that he's got to give it out. But in Sydney, if you watch the tape, you'll just see Richardson, Wessels and Brian McMillan jogging up to Donald.

'When the umpire doesn't give it, the reaction is almost one of, "Ach, well, it's our first game, let's go back to our positions and get on with it."

'As for the game itself, it was an amazing atmosphere with 45 000 people in the ground wondering who these upstarts from South Africa were. It was like Kepler Wessels and ten midgets trying to take on the World Champions in their own backyard! Kepler had got Alan Jones, the former Wallaby coach, to give us a motivational talk the night before and that was great.

'It was also the birth of Jonty Rhodes. He grabbed the headlines a few games later when he ran out Inzamam, but in this game there was a stop and a run-out at the bowler's end where both batsmen (Craig McDermott and Mike Whitney) froze in mid-pitch. They were so astonished by the length of the dive, the quickness of getting up and the release of the ball. It was an incredible moment.

'I bowled my first over in international cricket in that game and I subsequently saw the tape and heard what Garth le Roux had to say on the commentary. He watched me bowling a practice ball to mid-off and said, "I'm sure that Hansie wouldn't mind facing his own bowling!" Anyway, my first ball was a big inswinger (I swung the ball a lot at a very slow pace in those days) and it drifted down the leg-side and was called wide.

'I went for six in the over, which included a couple of overthrows, but my second over was a maiden and Garth said, "Hey, maybe he's got something here. Take the pace off, make it swing a bit, maybe he's OK". But Kepler got in on the act and he said that I'd never take more than the 18 wickets that he'd got at international level, but I did and I ended up with about 110.'

It was the perfect start for the South Africans and although they lost their next two matches, as the tournament progressed it became clear that they were not there just to make up the numbers. In Christchurch on 5 March they successfully defended 200 against the West Indies, largely due to some wonderful bowling from Meyrick Pringle, but it was their fifth game that really caught the public imagination, against Pakistan in Brisbane.

Benson & Hedges World Cup, 1991/92
Australia v South Africa
Sydney Cricket Ground (day/night)
26 February 1992 (50-overs match)

Result: South Africa won by 9 wickets

Australia innings
GR Marsh *c* Richardson *b* Kuiper..........25
DC Boon run out (Snell/Cronjé)..........27
DM Jones *c* Richardson *b* McMillan..........24
*AR Border *b* Kuiper..........0
TM Moody lbw *b* Donald..........10
SR Waugh *c* Cronjé *b* McMillan..........27
+IA Healy *c* McMillan *b* Donald..........16
PL Taylor *b* Donald..........4
CJ McDermott run out (Rhodes/Snell)..........6
MR Whitney not out..........9
BA Reid not out..........5
Extras (lb 2, w 11, nb 4)..........17
Total (9 wickets, 49 overs)..........170

FoW: 1-42 (Boon), 2-76 (Marsh), 3-76 (Border), 4-97 (Jones), 5-108 (Moody), 6-143 (Healy), 7-146 (Waugh), 8-156 (Taylor), 9-161 (McDermott).

Bowling	O	M	R	W
Donald	10	0	34	3
Pringle	10	0	52	0
Snell	9	1	15	0
McMillan	10	0	35	2
Kuiper	5	0	15	2
Cronjé	5	1	17	0

South Africa
*KC Wessels not out..........81
AC Hudson *b* Taylor..........28
PN Kirsten not out..........49
Extras (lb 5, w 6, nb 2)..........13
Total (1 wicket, 46.5 overs)..........171

DNB: WJ Cronjé, AP Kuiper, JN Rhodes, BM McMillan, +DJ Richardson, RP Snell, MW Pringle, AA Donald.

FoW: 1-74 (Hudson).

Bowling	O	M	R	W
McDermott	10	1	23	0
Reid	8.5	0	41	0
Whitney	6	0	26	0
Waugh	4	1	16	0
Taylor	10	1	32	1
Border	4	0	13	0

This one was given! A youthful Allan Donald races down the pitch to celebrate a wicket at the 1992 World Cup. As usual, Jonty Rhodes is the first man on the scene.
(Getty Images/Touchline Photo)

Kepler Wessels shakes the hand of Craig McDermott as South Africa clinch victory by nine wickets in their first World Cup match. Allan Border looks rueful, perhaps remembering that he had played Test cricket with Wessels for Australia in the days when South African sport was in isolation.
(Getty Images/Touchline Photo)

Jonty Rhodes Flies Into History

The performance of the South African team at the 1992 World Cup belied the acrimony that had preceded its departure from the republic. In the original squad of twenty the selectors had omitted three players who were regarded as essential to the health of the team. Clive Rice (42), Jimmy Cook (38) and Peter Kirsten (36) were all axed on the basis that they were too old, although Kirsten made it into the final squad and emerged as South Africa's best batsman.

The short tour to India had convinced the selectors that they had to pick athletic fielders if they were to compete, and principal among these was Jonathan Neil Rhodes, known to one and all as Jonty. Rhodes had an unorthodox batting technique, but the selectors believed that he was worth his place in the team just for his fielding, and so it proved. In the game against Pakistan he failed with the bat, but succeeded spectacularly in the field. He tells the story.

'It was still the league section, we batted first and got 211, which wasn't a very competitive total. We bowled well up front and then it rained and in those days the rain rule really favoured the side bowling second. When we came back out Pakistan needed 120 off 14.3 overs, the best part of eight and a half an over.

'Imran Khan and Inzamam ul Haq played so well that they were getting them easily from the first six or seven. There had been a huge downpour and the outfield and the ball were both wet. Our

'Hold whatever you're doing. I've got the front page picture.' The man who took this picture of Jonty Rhodes running out Inzamam ul Haq knew immediately that he'd got a classic.
(Courier Mail/Brisbane, Australia)

bowlers were struggling to grip the ball properly and we were rapidly losing the game. There were lots of boundaries because we were bowling full tosses in a failed attempt to bowl Yorkers.

'I was standing at point on the edge of the 30-metre circle, because we were happy at that stage to give away ones in an attempt to stop the fours. Brian McMillan was bowling and he hit Inzamam on the pad. I've seen the replay and it should probably have been given out, but it wasn't.

'I ran in and picked up the ball about halfway between the edge of the circle and the stumps and Inzamam's a big guy and I thought he was never going to get back. So I decided not to throw, but to run in and break the stumps and he actually surprised me because he got back a lot quicker than I was expecting.

'Now remember that this was before the third umpire system came in, so the decision had to be given by Steve Bucknor from his position at square leg. Looking back at it now it was brave call, even though it was the right one, because without the benefit of watching it on the TV replay it's the kind of judgement that used to be given to the batsman as benefit of the doubt.

'But it was given and it proved to be the turning point of the game. Two balls later Imran was caught behind and the game was as good as won. The next day we were leaving Brisbane to fly to our next game and there was my picture on the front page of the local newspaper. I spoke to the editor of the paper and he told me that the photographer phoned him as soon as it happened and said, "Hold whatever you're doing, I've got the front page picture."

'He hadn't even developed it and he had to find a tickey box to call his editor because that was before everyone had cellphones, but he knew he'd got an outstanding shot. He was shooting in black and white and there is a colour one taken by another photographer from a different angle, but it doesn't capture the moment half as well.

'The other Australian papers all picked it up and I thought it was a great picture, but that was all. I didn't think I'd done anything special. I didn't realise what an effect that one run-out had until I got home and went for my first haircut. My barber said to me, "You won't believe how many people have been in here asking for a Jonty Rhodes haircut."'

Ten years after Rhodes dived into history it's clear that this was no flash in the pan. Everywhere that South Africa play Rhodes has set new standards of fielding excellence. Other players hit the stumps more often, but none offer the constant threat he does. What marks him out is the pace of his recovery after first stopping the ball. The amount of ground he covers should be impossible, but having got there he then gets the ball into the danger areas better than anyone else, which is why after all this time batsmen are still being run out by him.

Benson & Hedges World Cup, 1991/92, 22nd Match
Pakistan v South Africa
Brisbane Cricket Ground, Woolloongabba
8 March 1992 (50-overs match)

Result: South Africa won by 20 runs (revised target)

South Africa innings
AC Hudson *c* Ijaz Ahmed *b* Imran Khan 54
*KC Wessels *c* Moin Khan *b* Aaqib Javed 7
MW Rushmere *c* Aamer Sohail *b* Mushtaq Ahmed...35
AP Kuiper *c* Moin Khan *b* Imran Khan 5
JN Rhodes lbw *b* Iqbal Sikander 5
WJ Cronjé not out 47
BM McMillan *b* Wasim Akram 33
+DJ Richardson *b* Wasim Akram 5
RP Snell not out 1
Extras (lb 8, w 9, nb 2) 19
Total (7 wickets, 50 overs) 211

DNB: MW Pringle, AA Donald.

FoW: 1-31 (Wessels), 2-98 (Hudson), 3-110 (Kuiper), 4-111 (Rushmere), 5-127 (Rhodes), 6-198 (McMillan), 7-207 (Richardson).

Bowling	O	M	R	W
Wasim Akram	10	0	42	2
Aaqib Javed	7	1	36	1
Imran Khan	10	0	34	2
Iqbal Sikander	8	0	30	1
Ijaz Ahmed	7	0	26	0
Mushtaq Ahmed	8	1	35	1

Pakistan innings (target: 194 runs from 36 overs)
Aamer Sohail *b* Snell 23
Zahid Fazal *c* Richardson *b* McMillan 11
Inzamam-ul-Haq run out (Rhodes) 48
*Imran Khan *c* Richardson *b* McMillan 34
Salim Malik *c* Donald *b* Kuiper 12
Wasim Akram *c* Snell *b* Kuiper 9
Ijaz Ahmed *c* Rhodes *b* Kuiper 6
+Moin Khan not out 5
Mushtaq Ahmed run out 4
Iqbal Sikander not out 1
Extras (lb 2, w 17, nb 1) 20
Total (8 wickets, 36 overs) 173

DNB: Aaqib Javed.

FoW: 1-50 (Aamer Sohail), 2-50 (Zahid Fazal), 3-135 (Inzamam-ul-Haq), 4-136 (Imran Khan), 5-156 (Salim Malik), 6-157 (Wasim Akram), 7-163 (Ijaz Ahmed), 8-171 (Mushtaq Ahmed).

Bowling	O	M	R	W
Donald	7	1	31	0
Pringle	7	0	31	0
Snell	8	2	26	1
McMillan	7	0	34	2
Kuiper	6	0	40	3
Cronjé	1	0	9	0

22 Runs Off One Ball

South Africa played eight log matches in only nineteen days at their first ever World Cup, winning five and losing three. They finished third on the log and had a week off to prepare for the semi-final against England in Sydney. England had won a desperately exciting log match against South Africa in Melbourne by three wickets with one ball to spare and, with a fine blend of allrounders and quality batsmen, were tipped as possible champions.

In Sydney, South Africa won the toss and put England in under gloomy skies. The start was delayed by half an hour due to rain and the floodlights were on from ball one. The trademark of South Africa's campaign had been their discipline in the field, with Rhodes' example lifting the ground fielding and the constant threat posed by Donald galvanising the bowlers.

Donald got rid of England captain Graham Gooch early and Brian McMillan broke a stump in clean bowling Ian Botham, but from 39 for two England began to get on top as the bowlers struggled with the damp ball. All the batsmen got a start, but it was Graeme Hick's 83 off 90 balls that held the innings together.

Searching for ways to stem the boundaries Wessels allowed his team to get behind on the over rate and the innings came to an end after only 45 of the 50 had been bowled with England on 252 for 6. A late flurry from Dermott Reeve made South Africa's task that much harder as he improvised his way to 25 not out off only 14 balls.

The frustrating end to South Africa's first World Cup. Rain drove the players from the field with South Africa needing a further 22 runs to win off the last 13 balls. The rain stopped falling almost as soon as the last player had reached the dressing room, but the rules of the competition were inflexible and, in a decision based largely on television scheduling, the statisticians had the final say. Instead of requiring 22 off 13 balls, South Africa's revised target was 21 off one. The stadium scoreboard flashed up incorrectly '22 off 1 ball' and a chorus of boos echoed around the ground. Brian McMillan is about to take strike, Dave Richardson is at the other end, England wicketkeeper Alec Stewart looks nonchalantly on.
(Getty Images/Touchline Photo)

The tournament is over; let's call it a day. England captain Graham Gooch commiserates with Brian McMillan after the final ball of the second semi-final of the 1992 World Cup. Rain robbed the SCG crowd of a wonderful climax and South Africa were denied a shot at final glory in their first World Cup.
(Getty Images/Touchline Photo)

Rain fell again during the supper break, but the South African reply started on time, needing 253 to win in 45 overs. Wessels went early and at various stages just as the batsmen seemed set, a wicket would fall to restore the equilibrium. The key innings came from Rhodes who made 43 off 38 balls to bring the target down to 46 from the last five overs.

The seventh-wicket pair, Richardson and McMillan, had scored 14 off two overs when Chris Lewis came on to bowl the 43rd over. Rain began to fall at the beginning of it and suddenly the prospect of a major upset became apparent. Lewis struggled to grip the wet ball, Richardson and McMillan swung lustily and 10 further runs had been gathered off five deliveries when the umpires decided that conditions were unfit for play and sent the teams to the dressing room.

At that gripping juncture South Africa's target had been reduced to 22 runs off 13 balls. Philip DeFreitas who, with one for 28 from eight overs had proved England's best bowler on the day, would have bowled the 44th over. But Lewis had conceded 38 off five and, with Botham, Gladstone Small and Richard Illingworth all having completed their allocation of 10 overs, it would have been down to the fragile Lewis to bowl the last.

The players, the crowd and an enchanted international television audience of untold millions, all knew that this was a contest that could go either way. A couple of wickets and England would wrap it up, but if Richardson and McMillan could somehow get the target down to 10 or 12 off the last over South Africa had a real chance.

The rain stopped falling almost as soon as the last player had reached the dressing room, but the rules of the competition were inflexible and, in a decision based largely on television scheduling, the statisticians had the final say. Instead of requiring 22 off 13 balls, South Africa's revised target was 21 off one. The stadium scoreboard flashed up incorrectly '22 off 1 ball' and a chorus of boos echoed around the ground.

Rules were rules, but this was the World Cup semi-final. It should have been played to a finish, but instead as the players got back into place, McMillan offered a dead bat to Lewis' final delivery and a most unsatisfactory conclusion had been reached. The long-term effect of it was to change the rules for subsequent World Cups, but that did not make it any easier to bear for a gallant South African team who had been eliminated from the competition at the final hurdle.

For Donald, Cronjé and Rhodes, all of whom went on to great things in ODI cricket, it was a moment that came back to haunt them when, seven years later, they once again found themselves part of a team that had reached the semi-final of the World Cup, this time the 1999 tournament in England.

Benson & Hedges World Cup, 1991/92, 2nd Semi-final
England v South Africa
Sydney Cricket Ground (day/night)
22 March 1992 (50-overs match)

Result: England won by 19 runs (revised target)

England innings (45 overs maximum)

*GA Gooch c Richardson b Donald	2
IT Botham b Pringle	21
+AJ Stewart c Richardson b McMillan	33
GA Hick c Rhodes b Snell	83
NH Fairbrother b Pringle	28
AJ Lamb c Richardson b Donald	19
CC Lewis not out	18
DA Reeve not out	25
Extras (b 1, lb 7, w 9, nb 6)	23
Total (6 wickets, 45 overs)	**252**

DNB: PAJ DeFreitas, GC Small, RK Illingworth.

FoW: 1-20 (Gooch), 2-39 (Botham), 3-110 (Stewart), 4-183 (Fairbrother), 5-187 (Hick), 6-221 (Lamb).

Bowling	O	M	R	W
Donald	10	0	69	2
Pringle	9	2	36	2
Snell	8	0	52	1
McMillan	9	0	47	1
Kuiper	5	0	26	0
Cronjé	4	0	14	0

South Africa innings
(target: 252 runs from 43 overs)

*KC Wessels c Lewis b Botham	17
AC Hudson lbw b Illingworth	46
PN Kirsten b DeFreitas	11
AP Kuiper b Illingworth	36
WJ Cronjé c Hick b Small	24
JN Rhodes c Lewis b Small	43
BM McMillan not out	21
+DJ Richardson not out	13
Extras (lb 17, w 4)	21
Total (6 wickets, 43 overs)	**232**

DNB: RP Snell, MW Pringle, AA Donald.

FoW: 1-26 (Wessels), 2-61 (Kirsten), 3-90 (Hudson), 4-131 (Kuiper), 5-176 (Cronjé), 6-206 (Rhodes).

Bowling	O	M	R	W
Botham	10	0	52	1
Lewis	5	0	38	0
DeFreitas	8	1	28	1
Illingworth	10	1	46	2
Small	10	1	51	2

It would be easy to say that in 1999 South Africa peaked too early, but that would be to ignore the efforts of Lance Klusener. The Natal allrounder ended the tournament with 281 runs, which may have been only the twelfth highest aggregate, but the fact that they were scored in pressure situations off just 230 balls, ensured that there was only one choice for the player of the tournament award.

Against Sri Lanka in Northampton, South Africa were 122 for eight when Steve Elworthy joined Klusener. With eight balls of the innings remaining Klusener was 25 not out. He then hit Sanath Jayasuriya for a four and a single to keep the strike for the final over bowled by Chaminda Vaas. A two, two fours and two sixes off the left-arm seamer brought the innings to a close with 22 off the final over. Klusener was 52 not out off 45 balls.

In the Super Six section South Africa needed 45 off 33 balls against Pakistan when Mark Boucher joined Klusener. This time he finished 46 not out off 41 balls with three fours and three sixes. In gloomy conditions bowlers of the quality of Wasim Akram and the sheer pace of Shoaib Akhtar were dealt with as if they were club medium pacers.

Klusener's remarkable form lasted another twelve months, but the inevitable lean spell came in 2001/2 and he actually lost his place in the team for a while. But against Australia in South Africa in 2002 he regained his confidence and returned to his best. During the lean spell his technique was questioned, but that was rather like criticising a swan for not being a goose. Hansie Cronjé always believed that Klusener is a lot more orthodox than most people think.

This time not even Lance Klusener, the patron saint of lost causes, can save South Africa. Klusener made 52 not out against Zimbabwe in Chelmsford and here he hits one of his two sixes, but South Africa still finished 48 runs short.
(Duif du Toit/Touchline Photo)

The most intimidating sight for any bowler at the 1999 World Cup was Lance Klusener in full flow. Hansie Cronjé describes his method: 'He is incredibly strong, but when he's playing well he hits it straight, a little bit like Ian Botham used to. He only practises with a bowling machine and he practises to hit it straight back past the bowler. And when he gets his timing right he has this big bat and it comes on to the ball with such force that he'll hit it past boundary fielders even if they've only got a couple of yards to move.'
(Duif du Toit/Touchline Photo)

The amazing Lance Klusener pulls Pakistan's Shoaib Akhtar for six. Akhtar had helped reduce South Africa to 58 for five, and when he came back in fading light South Africa still needed 45 off just 34 balls. Klusener's response was to take 17 runs off his comeback over and South Africa won a match they seemed certain to lose with an over to spare.
(Duif du Toit/Touchline Photo)

He said: 'I realised this guy was something special right at the start of the 1999 World Cup. We played India in Hove and they got a handsome total. We were going OK, but Jacques Kallis got out and when Lance came in we needed 27 off 26 balls. The first ball he received from Ajit Agarkar, who was bowling quick at the time, was a perfect half-volley and he hit it over mid-on's head up the hill and it picked up pace when it bounced, hit a spectator in the chest and knocked him straight over the back of his deck chair!

'Jacques and I had really battled to get the ball away on that pitch, but I realised then that Lance just had an incredible talent and he hit his first three balls for four to effectively settle the match. In the penultimate over of the Pakistan game Shoaib Akhtar bowled him a bouncer and he hooked it into the stands for six; what was impressive was how quickly the ball travelled.

'He is incredibly strong, but when he's playing well he hits it straight, a little bit like Ian Botham used to. He only practises with a bowling machine and he practises to hit it straight back past the bowler. And when he gets his timing right he has this big bat and it comes on to the ball with such force that he'll hit it past boundary fielders even if they've only got a couple of yards to move.'

Which brings us to the match considered by many as the greatest game of one-day cricket ever played.

Allan Donald acknowledges the remarkable talent of Lance Klusener with a tap on the helmet. In the final over of South Africa's 1999 World Cup match against Sri Lanka in Northampton, Klusener hit Chaminda Vaas for four, two, four, dot, six, six.
(Duif du Toit/Touchline Photo)

Just in case anyone had forgotten. Lance Klusener's heroics with the bat won him the man of the tournament award at the 1999 World Cup, but when first selected he was a fast bowler good enough to take eight for 64 on his Test debut against India.
(Duif du Toit/Touchline Photo)

Allan Donald's Run-out

After winning their first five games, South Africa got complacent and lost to Zimbabwe in Chelmsford. That meant that they only took two points through to the Super Six section rather than four, because Zimbabwe qualified at the expense of England, one of the teams that South Africa had blown away in log play.

Against Australia in their final Super Six game at Headingley, South Africa could not defend 271 for seven, so they were forced to play the same team in the second semi-final at Edgbaston, the ground where Allan Donald had forged his reputation playing for Warwickshire in the isolation years.

Cronjé said that losing in Leeds 'was a huge psychological blow to us ahead of the semi-final especially the fact that they had successfully chased 270 and that Steve Waugh and Shane Warne, who had both had poor tournaments up to then, had got themselves into form. Warne got three wickets and bowled well and Waugh got a big hundred and they both emerged as key players in the semi-final.

'If we had played either New Zealand or Pakistan (the other semi-finalists) I think we would have won, but we had only ourselves to blame because we played poorly against Zimbabwe in the Super Six section and lost by a heavy margin that affected our overall run rate.'

Put into bat, Australia made 213 from 49.2 overs. They had seemed set for more when Waugh and Michael Bevan put on 90 for the fifth wicket, but Donald and Shaun Pollock came back to blow the tail away. Australia lost their last four wickets for six runs.

The moment that changed the momentum of the match came in the 11th over of South Africa's reply when Waugh called Warne up to bowl with still five overs to go before fielding restrictions could be lifted. South Africa had reached 48 without loss when Warne began his second over with a delivery only he among contemporary players was capable of, bowling Herschelle Gibbs for 30.

Cronjé said: 'The ball that Warne got Gibbs with has been compared to the one he got Mike Gatting with in a Test match and it's hard to criticise the batsman. All right, Herschelle shouldn't have been trying to hit him through the leg-side, but when Warnie's on song he makes you do that because he drifts the ball so much that you get yourself into an awkward position.'

Warne then bowled Gary Kirsten for 18 and had Cronjé caught at slip for a duck, although television replays showed that the ball had come off the South African captain's toe, rather than the bat. From 48 for none it had become 53 for three and when Daryll Cullinan was run out by a direct hit from extra cover by Bevan it was 61 for four. After a promising start it was back to square one.

Rhodes and Kallis dug in and, without ever suggesting dominance, they got South Africa back into the game with a stand worth 84. The South African motto for the tournament was 'one run can make a difference' and Cronjé remembers a moment during this stand where it was etched in sharp relief.

'A defining moment in the game was when Jonty hit Glen McGrath towards the boundary, but he hit it so high that when it hit the ground it plugged and instead of running into the boundary it just stopped. They were able to save two runs and that came back to haunt us.'

In the 40th over Rhodes mistimed a pull against Paul Reiffel and was caught at deep square leg. Now 69 runs were required off 57 balls with five wickets in hand. Warne's figures were dented slightly by Pollock who smashed 20 off 14 balls, but his penultimate delivery accounted for Jacques Kallis and when Klusener joined Pollock 39 were needed off 31 balls.

Amid almost unbearable tension Pollock, stepping back to give himself room, was bowled by Damien Fleming. Next, Mark Boucher was bowled by McGrath for five and in a quest to give Klusener the strike Steve Elworthy was run out for a single, bringing in last man Allan Donald. Cronjé takes up the story.

Steve Waugh begins the end game. Dropped on 56, Waugh went on to score a match-winning century.
(Getty Images/Touchline Photo)

ICC World Cup, 1999, 2nd Semi-final
Australia v South Africa
Edgbaston, Birmingham
17 June 1999 (50-over match)

Result: Match tied

Australia innings
+AC Gilchrist c Donald b Kallis 20
ME Waugh c Boucher b Pollock 0
RT Ponting c Kirsten b Donald 37
DS Lehmann c Boucher b Donald 1
*SR Waugh c Boucher b Pollock 56
MG Bevan c Boucher b Pollock 65
TM Moody lbw b Pollock 0
SK Warne c Cronjé b Pollock 18
PR Reiffel b Donald 0
DW Fleming b Donald 0
GD McGrath not out 0
Extras (b 1, lb 6, w 3, nb 6) 16
Total (all out, 49.2 overs) 213

FoW: 1-3 (ME Waugh), 2-54 (Ponting), 3-58 (Lehmann), 4-68 (Gilchrist), 5-158 (SR Waugh), 6-158 (Moody), 7-207 (Warne), 8-207 (Reiffel), 9-207 (Fleming), 10-213 (Bevan).

Bowling	O	M	R	W
Pollock	9.2	1	36	5
Elworthy	10	0	59	0
Kallis	10	2	27	1
Donald	10	1	32	4
Klusener	9	1	50	0
Cronjé	1	0	2	0

South Africa innings
G Kirsten b Warne 18
HH Gibbs b Warne 30
DJ Cullinan run out (Bevan) 6
*WJ Cronjé c ME Waugh b Warne 0
JH Kallis c SR Waugh b Warne 53
JN Rhodes c Bevan b Reiffel 43
SM Pollock b Fleming 20
L Klusener not out 31
+MV Boucher b McGrath 5
S Elworthy run out (Reiffel/McGrath) 1
AA Donald run out (Fleming/Gilchrist) 0
Extras (lb 1, w 5) 6
Total (all out, 49.4 overs) 213

FoW: 1-48 (Gibbs), 2-53 (Kirsten), 3-53 (Cronjé), 4-61 (Cullinan), 5-145 (Rhodes), 6-175 (Kallis), 7-183 (Pollock), 8-196 (Boucher), 9-198 (Elworthy), 10-213 (Donald).

Bowling	O	M	R	W
McGrath	10	0	51	1
Fleming	8.4	1	40	1
Reiffel	8	0	28	1
Warne	10	4	29	4
ME Waugh	8	0	37	0
Moody	5	0	27	0

Contrasting emotions for Herschelle Gibbs. Here he celebrates his dashing century against Australia in the final match of the Super Six section at Headingley in the 1999 World Cup. Gibbs made 101 from 134 balls with 10 fours and a six.
(Duif du Toit/Touchline Photo)

But in the picture on the right Gibbs seems to be contemplating the dropped catch that may have cost his country the World Cup. Steve Waugh, on 56, hit a routine catch off Lance Klusener to Gibbs at midwicket. In the act of catching and celebrating Gibbs dropped the ball. Waugh is supposed to have said, 'Well done, mate, you've just dropped the World Cup.' The Australian captain went on to score 120 not out and Australia won the game by five wickets. Gibbs walked into a media storm after the game and this picture was taken at practice a few days later. Nicky Boje is the other face behind designer shades.
(Duif du Toit/Touchline Photo)

'So after the late collapse we needed 16 off the last eight balls and I didn't give us any chance, but Lance hit a six through Paul Reiffel's hands on the boundary and got a single off the next to keep the strike for the last over (nine needed). Whenever Lance is batting Shaun Pollock has a knack of forecasting what he's going to do and he picked the spot where he was going to hit it.

'The first boundary went just wide of Mark Waugh on the extra cover boundary for four and it was the power in the shot that really stood out. Mark Waugh's quick and he only had to move the length of a couple of advertising boards, but by the time Lance had said "Yes" the ball was already over the boundary.

'The next one went past cover for four and with the scores tied there was a bit of genius from whoever suggested that Fleming should go back over the wicket. He had been round when the two fours were hit, but then went over and bowled the perfect Yorker, the one where Allan was nearly run out.'

Donald, at the non-striker's end, would have been run out by two metres if Darren Lehmann's throw had hit the stumps and that was at the front of his mind when Klusener hit the next ball back past him and called for a single.

In the confusion that followed, Donald turned to regain his ground, looked up to see Klusener past the point of no return, dropped his bat and was left stranded as Mark Waugh picked up the ball and returned it to Fleming, who relayed it to wicketkeeper Adam Gilchrist to break the stumps and end the innings with the scores tied. Australia progressed to the final by dint of the fact that they had finished above South Africa on run rate in the Super Six section.

At the beginning of the tournament coach Bob Woolmer had experimented with two-way communication between the field and the dressing room through earpieces connected to a radio transmitter. But during South Africa's first game the ICC banned the idea, a move that Cronjé feels might have had an effect on the destination of the trophy.

With two balls left in the match Steve Waugh (facing page) has hit the winning runs off Shaun Pollock to get his team into the World Cup semi-finals against the same opponents. Waugh said that he had never played better in his distinguished career. He finished 120 not out off 110 balls with 10 fours and two sixes.
(Getty Images/Touchline Photo)

Allan Donald is almost exactly halfway down the pitch as Adam Gilchrist breaks the stumps to end the 1999 World Cup semi-final between South Africa and Australia.
(Getty Images/Touchline Photo)

A remarkable photograph by Ross Kinaird of Getty Images captures the moment that no South African will ever forget. Allan Donald is run out going for the winning run in the 1999 World Cup semi-final at Edgbaston. The only participant in the final over drama missing from this image is Lance Klusener, who was already halfway to the pavilion. From left: Adam Gilchrist, Mark Waugh, Darren Lehmann, Damien Fleming, Glen McGrath, Michael Bevan, Steve Waugh, Ricky Ponting, Shane Warne, Tom Moody, Allan Donald, Paul Reiffel. Umpire Venkat, apparently oblivious to the drama, stoops to remove the bails and officially end the match. To his right is Donald's bat, dropped as he belatedly responded to Klusener's call.
(Getty Images/Touchline Photo)

'I've often thought since that moment what might have happened if we had been allowed to use earpieces. It would have been the perfect opportunity for Bob to calm everything down from the dressing room by telling Allan to let Lance try and hit a boundary and to run only if the scores were still tied on the last ball.'

But according to Rhodes, the real reason for the defeat was Cronjé himself. He said: 'There's a superstition in the team that if you're sitting somewhere and a partnership develops you don't get out of your seat. You don't go to the toilet, you don't have a drink, you just sit there. Well, Hansie had been sitting down all the time that Lance was winning the game and when he hit his second boundary he got up to go to the door so that he would be able to run on to the field and congratulate him.

'The whole of South Africa knows what happened next. It still plagues me, but I did an article recently with questions about my favourite and least favourite things and there was a question that said what is the worst thing you've been forgiven for. I haven't done too many bad things in my life, so that wasn't a problem, but the next question was, what's the worst thing you have forgiven someone else for and I wrote, "Allan Donald dropping his bat and not making it for one."'

South African captain Hansie Cronjé tries to calm his team during a tense moment in the 1999 World Cup.
(Getty Images/Touchline Photo)

Perhaps due to the number of their players who campaigned for English counties, Pakistan adapted to ODI cricket a lot earlier than their great rivals, India. They were helped by the emergence in the mid-70s of two of the greatest cricketers of all time, Javed Miandad and Imran Khan.

Miandad was one of the great innovators. When, towards the end of the 1980s, captains gambled with their field placing by bringing fine leg up inside the 30-metre circle, Miandad would walk across his stumps and flick balls from outside off stump, past fine leg to the boundary. It has become a commonplace stroke, with even tail-enders adept at playing it these days, but Miandad was the genius who showed the way.

In the 1970s the great South African batsman Barry Richards developed the art of moving outside leg stump and hitting the ball over extra cover. That too seems commonplace today, but there is no mention of it in the MCC coaching manual and it was certainly never played by the generations who were brought up on three, four and five-day cricket.

Miandad can also lay claim to first perfecting and then popularising the one shot that can still be relied upon to bring criticism down from the commentary box, the reverse sweep. It can truly be said that without Miandad's example, Mike Gatting would never have attempted the reverse sweep in the 1987 World Cup final that changed the whole course of the match. The difference between Gatting and Miandad was that, while both fell to the reverse sweep in a World Cup final, when Miandad got out against England in 1992 Pakistan's platform for victory had been well and truly laid.

Miandad played county cricket first for Sussex and later for Glamorgan. It was in this second spell that he did something that causes wry smiles of disbelief to this day. The former Middlesex and England seamer Mike Selvey, now a respected journalist, captained Glamorgan. Selvey swears that during the course of a Miandad century the fielding captain, for whom all other tactics had failed, loaded the boundary with fielders in order to give Miandad one and get him off strike.

Miandad's response was to start inside edging the ball on to his pads, from whence it would loop up in the air towards the non-existent short leg or silly point. After a few overs of this the fielding captain became convinced that the ball was turning and that Miandad was in trouble, so he brought the field in and surrounded the batsman. At which point Miandad lashed the ball to all parts of the boundary, now blissfully vacant. Such mastery is given to but few and, if Viv Richards was a more destructive player than Miandad, then it was Richards himself who said that if he wanted someone to bat for his life it would be Miandad.

Javed Miandad liked to work the ball around, but he was not averse to hitting over the top if the situation demanded it. Former New Zealand captain Ken Rutherford had this to say about Miandad: 'He was very keen to be heard and was totally enthusiastic about informing the bowler how useless he was and suggesting to the fielding captain where the fielders should be situated. He would work the bowlers into a tizz, pushing the ball into certain areas and then unleashing the big shots once his favoured zone was vacant. Very annoying to play against, but it's hard not to admire his skill.'
(Getty Images/Touchline Photo)

Ken Rutherford, the former New Zealand captain, calls Miandad 'simply a genius of the run chase. In a final in Sharjah Pakistan needed 4 runs to win off the last ball. Miandad, already on 110 not out, whipped a leg-side full toss from the hapless Chetan Sharma into the stands to send the Pakistani fans delirious. Sitting back in my hotel room watching this drama unfold was a splendid way to while away the day.'

But as is frequently the case with geniuses in many walks of life, Miandad's social skills were a little underdeveloped. As a result he was never a good captain and it took the much more authoritarian methods of Imran Khan to bring out the best in Pakistan. Under Imran, Pakistan played as a team; without him they were frequently just eleven individuals, many of whom didn't particularly like each other.

Imran dabbled with retirement on several occasions, but his swansong turned out to be the 1992 World Cup. By then he was not the ferocious paceman of the 1980s, though he was still a fine bowler, but he had developed his batting and was particularly adept at scoring runs when they really mattered.

But even with these two champion cricketers, looking back at the 1992 World Cup it is almost impossible to believe that Pakistan won it. They lost their first match by 10 wickets against the West Indies, were bowled out for 74 by England in Adelaide only to be saved by the rain and, in all, lost three and had one no result in their first five games. It is in circumstances such as these that volatile teams – and there has never been a Pakistan side short of volatility – tend to implode. Instead they went unbeaten for their next six games and won the tournament. As they say in America, go figure.

Wasim Akram in the 1992 World Cup Final

This was the third time that England had reached the World Cup Final and poor Graham Gooch, captain this time around, played in and lost all three. In 1979 it was due to the brilliance of the West Indies team under Clive Lloyd, in 1987 it was a moment of madness from Mike Gatting, but in 1992 they were a good side who just ran into an irresistible force.

Many things contributed to Pakistan's victory, but three names stand out: Imran Khan, Javed Miandad and Wasim Akram. In a tournament in which he had batted down the order and not contributed a single half-century, Imran promoted himself to number three in the final and top scored with 72. He correctly surmised that what was really needed was a clear head and from the depths of 24 for two he masterminded a total of 249 for six.

Imran and Miandad toiled for 31 overs in adding 139 for the third wicket. Miandad was eventually out for 58 made from 98 balls with only four boundaries. In a tournament in which he had scarcely failed it was his most dour, yet most important, innings. Imran was equally parsimonious, making his runs from 110 balls with five fours and a six and when he was out Pakistan were 197 for four in the 44th over, still some way short of a competitive score.

Richard Illingworth: caught Rameez Raja, bowled Imran Khan 14. The last pair put on 19 for England, but with four balls left in the innings the captain wrapped up proceedings to give Pakistan the 1992 World Cup.
(Getty Images/Touchline Photo)

Wasim Akram (left) and Javed Miandad give in to the delirium of winning the World Cup.
(Getty Images/Touchline Photo)

Javed Miandad was the only man to play in every one of the first five World Cups and he crowned his remarkable career with victory in 1992. Here he is on his way to 58 against England in the final, building a platform for the later assault by Inzamam-ul-Haq and Wasim Akram.
(Getty Images/Touchline Photo)

**Benson & Hedges World Cup, 1992, Final
England v Pakistan
Melbourne Cricket Ground (day/night)**
25 March 1992 (50-overs match)

Result: Pakistan won by 22 runs

Pakistan innings
Aamer Sohail c Stewart b Pringle 4
Rameez Raja lbw b Pringle 8
*Imran Khan c Illingworth b Botham 72
Javed Miandad c Botham b Illingworth 58
Inzamam-ul-Haq b Pringle 42
Wasim Akram run out 33
Salim Malik not out 0
Extras (lb 19, w 6, nb 7) 32
Total (6 wickets, 50 overs) 249

DNB: Ijaz Ahmed, +Moin Khan, Mushtaq Ahmed, Aaqib Javed.

FoW: 1-20 (Aamer Sohail), 2-24 (Rameez Raja), 3-163 (Javed Miandad), 4-197 (Imran Khan), 5-249 (Inzamam-ul-Haq), 6-249 (Wasim Akram).

Bowling	O	M	R	W
Pringle	10	2	22	3
Lewis	10	2	52	0
Botham	7	0	42	1
DeFreitas	10	1	42	0
Illingworth	10	0	50	1
Reeve	3	0	22	0

England innings
*GA Gooch c Aaqib Javed b Mushtaq Ahmed 29
IT Botham c Moin Khan b Wasim Akram 0
+AJ Stewart c Moin Khan b Aaqib Javed 7
GA Hick lbw b Mushtaq Ahmed 17
NH Fairbrother c Moin Khan b Aaqib Javed 62
AJ Lamb b Wasim Akram 31
CC Lewis b Wasim Akram 0
DA Reeve c Rameez Raja b Mushtaq Ahmed 15
DR Pringle not out 18
PAJ DeFreitas run out 10
RK Illingworth c Rameez Raja b Imran Khan 14
Extras (lb 5, w 13, nb 6) 24
Total (all out, 49.2 overs) 227

FoW: 1-6 (Botham), 2-21 (Stewart), 3-59 (Hick), 4-69 (Gooch), 5-141 (Lamb), 6-141 (Lewis), 7-180 (Fairbrother), 8-183 (Reeve), 9-208 (DeFreitas), 10-227 (Illingworth).

Bowling	O	M	R	W
Wasim Akram	10	0	49	3
Aaqib Javed	10	2	27	2
Mushtaq Ahmed	10	1	41	3
Ijaz Ahmed	3	0	13	0
Imran Khan	6.2	0	43	1
Aamer Sohail	10	0	49	0

But Imran and Miandad had laid the foundation, allowing the lower middle order to take the bowling by the scruff of the neck. Inzamam-ul-Haq clouted 42 off 35 balls and Wasim Akram an audacious 33 off just 19. The pair put on 52 for the fifth wicket in six overs and swung the game decisively in Pakistan's favour. The batsmen had done their job, now it was down to the bowlers.

Again, Imran's captaincy was a key aspect. He had a fine attack, but the ace in the hole was Akram. The left-arm paceman bowled five overs with the new ball and had Ian Botham caught behind in his second. He had one for 25 from five when Imran removed him and began to juggle his options, bringing the leg-spin of Mushtaq Ahmed on early and also experimenting with the left-arm spin of Aamer Sohail. He did not give himself a bowl until the 27th over.

Imran's concern was the batting depth of England, who could boast Philip DeFreitas at number 10 and Richard Illingworth at number 11, both of whom had first class centuries to their name. Among the top order there was a fine balance of workers and strikers and Mushtaq did much for the confidence of the team by dismissing Gooch and Graeme Hick in his first spell to reduce England to 69 for four.

Javed Miandad (57 not out) hits the winning run against New Zealand in the 1992 World Cup semi-final in Auckland. Pakistan successfully overhauled New Zealand's impressive 262 for seven and with Miandad, the master of the run chase, guiding the innings, did so with an over to spare.
(Getty Images/Touchline Photo)

Imran Khan with the 1992 World Cup trophy.
(Getty Images/Touchline Photo)

But inevitably there had to be a partnership and it came now in the contrasting styles of Neil Fairbrother and Allan Lamb. Fairbrother was a left-hander from Lancashire who was the master of the run chase in domestic cricket, running balls either side of cover with an angled bat and sprinting between the wickets as if his life depended on it. Lamb was at the end of his career, a savage square cutter who was particularly effective against fast bowling.

The pair were a fine contrast and they slowly edged England back into the game. Then in the 35th over Imran pulled his masterstroke, recalling Akram to the attack. In his autobiography, Lamb is the master of understatement as to what happened next. He said: 'I was going well with 31 and so was Fairbrother and we had put on 72 in 14 overs when back came Wasim Akram and he bowled me and Chris Lewis with two bananas in two balls and Pakistan went on to win by 22 runs.'

Put like that it seems very matter of fact, but it was hardly that. What actually happened was that Akram, struggling to control the swing of the white ball from over the wicket, went round. For any ordinary left-arm seamer this should provide no problem for two batsmen well set. It meant that, with Akram bowling from the extremity of the crease, lbw was more or less out of the question and it should also have removed any chance of the ball swinging away from the right-hander.

After the dust had settled Imran Khan was reunited with the trophy for a more demure picture.
(Getty Images/Touchline Photo)

Wasim Akram celebrates the key breakthrough in the 1992 World Cup final. With England well placed at 141 for five, Akram decided to go around the wicket from where he slanted the ball in to and then swung it away from an astonished Allan Lamb, who was bowled for 31.
(Getty Images/Touchline Photo)

In the whole history of the game there has never been a left-arm bowler of genuine pace (as opposed to medium-pace) who has been able to swing the ball away from the right-hander from around the wicket. Allan Davidson, the great Australian left-armer of the 1950s certainly didn't do it, and he is the only man who can really stand comparison with Akram as the best of his type ever.

Akram changed the course of the match in two balls by doing what was apparently impossible. The ball that got Lamb was bowled from wide of the crease, pitched on middle stump and hit off. Lamb walked off shaking his head. He was in and playing well and could not put a bat on it. What chance was there for a new batsman? None at all, as it turned out, and Lewis' dismissal made it 141 for six. Fairbrother fought on with the tail, but despite some late hitting from Derek Pringle and DeFreitas, England's chance had gone, blown away by Akram's golden moment.

Facing page: Wasim Akram dismisses Ian Botham for a duck in the 1992 World Cup final. Botham had been used as an opener by England during the tournament and had given them a number of excellent starts with his ability to hit over the top of the infield. In the final he met his match against an allrounder from a younger generation.
(Getty Images/Touchline Photo)

Another express delivery from Wasim Akram eludes the bat of Derek Pringle, eliciting a full-throated roar. Pringle survived, making 18 not out and with some lusty blows took England close, but not close enough.
(Getty Images/Touchline Photo)

Waqar Younis Destroys South Africa

The year after winning the World Cup Pakistan made history by touring South Africa for the first time. They played in a triangular one-day series with the West Indies and, while they had to do without Imran who had retired, they were able to include Waqar Younis, the pace bowler who had missed the World Cup because of injury. Learning from Imran, Younis mastered the art of high pace reverse swing and left a trail of batsmen in his wake with crushed toes, deflated egos and shattered stumps.

The great Waqar Younis bowling in the 1996 World Cup. Head steady, body balanced, a fast bowler with control, not just pace.
(Getty Images/Touchline Photo)

Akram took over the captaincy and both he and Younis relished bowling on South African pitches. They took it in turns to humiliate the home nation and Hansie Cronjé remembers vividly the day that Younis, with an analysis of 10-0-25-5, transformed a match in Durban.

'I was batting number four, Andrew Hudson and Kepler Wessels had put on 101 for the first wicket and when Peter Kirsten got out and I went in it was 159 for two. I had been padded up all that time watching them hit Mushtaq Ahmed and all the other bowlers to all parts of the ground. We needed 50 off 10 overs when I came in, the weather had just become a little grey as it does towards evening in Durban, and Wasim and Waqar had five overs each left to bowl.

'It was a day game and we used a red ball and at that time the only reverse swing we had seen was at the World Cup and then, because of the two white balls it wasn't proper reverse, because it was still a relatively new ball. In Durban I faced the fastest and most accurate bowling of my whole career.

'It was one of those days when Wasim was actually quicker than Waqar, which wasn't normally the case. Wasim has a quick arm action, which makes it difficult to sight the ball. Later on Clive Rice gave me a tip about spotting the shiny side in the bowler's hand before it's released so you know which way it's going to go, but this was only my eighth or ninth game and I was very naïve.

'The bowling was accurate, aggressive and deadly; it was everything that we had not been exposed to during isolation and from needing five an over with eight wickets in hand we lost by 10 runs. To cap it off, the next game was in East London and they did the same again. We wanted 25 off five with seven in hand that time and didn't get close. They both bowled straight and hit the stumps and got lbws.

'The lesson that we learned in later years was that you can't bat the traditional way against teams with good reverse swing in the final overs. Wasim and Waqar were always going to be effective at the end. What you've got to do is get runs in the middle period and at the start so that you're ahead of the clock when the ball starts to reverse.

'Wasim went round the wicket (like he did in the World Cup final) to me a few times in county cricket when he was playing for Lancashire and I was with Leicestershire. He would swing the ball away and then put in the odd Yorker as variation. He is right up there in any discussion of the greatest one-day cricketers because not only could he change the course of the match with either bat or ball, but he's got a good head on his shoulders.'

Total International Series, 1992/93, 1st Match
South Africa v Pakistan
Kingsmead, Durban
9 February 1993 (50-overs match)

Result: Pakistan won by 10 runs

Pakistan innings
Saeed Anwar b Donald	0
Rameez Raja c Richardson b Matthews	29
Inzamam-ul-Haq run out (McMillan)	47
Javed Miandad c Richardson b McMillan	22
Salim Malik c McMillan b Cronjé	14
Asif Mujtaba not out	49
+Rashid Latif c Richardson b McMillan	15
*Wasim Akram not out	20
Extras (lb 10, w 2)	12
Total (6 wickets, 50 overs)	**208**

DNB: Waqar Younis, Mushtaq Ahmed, Aaqib Javed.

FoW: 1-0 (Saeed Anwar), 2-46 (Rameez Raja), 3-93 (Inzamam-ul-Haq), 4-107 (Javed Miandad), 5-132 (Salim Malik), 6-166 (Rashid Latif).

Bowling	O	M	R	W
Donald	10	2	32	1
de Villiers	10	0	41	0
Matthews	10	0	54	1
McMillan	10	1	35	2
Cronjé	10	0	36	1

South Africa innings
AC Hudson b Waqar Younis	93
*KC Wessels lbw b Wasim Akram	42
PN Kirsten b Asif Mujtaba	18
WJ Cronjé b Waqar Younis	11
DJ Cullinan b Waqar Younis	0
JN Rhodes run out (Rashid Latif)	5
BM McMillan run out (Wasim Akram)	2
+DJ Richardson run out (Javed Miandad)	11
CR Matthews b Waqar Younis	3
PS de Villiers b Waqar Younis	1
AA Donald not out	1
Extras (lb 7, w 1, nb 3)	11
Total (all out, 50 overs)	**198**

FoW: 1-101 (Wessels), 2-159 (Kirsten), 3-165 (Hudson), 4-165 (Cullinan), 5-180 (Cronjé), 6-182 (McMillan), 7-182 (Rhodes), 8-195 (Matthews), 9-197 (Richardson), 10-198 (de Villiers).

Bowling	O	M	R	W
Wasim Akram	10	1	36	1
Aaqib Javed	10	1	38	0
Mushtaq Ahmed	10	0	46	0
Waqar Younis	10	0	25	5
Asif Mujtaba	10	1	46	1

Shahid Afridi's Match

If I were to pick just one match from all of the magic moments contained in this book, one match to encompass the thrill of the one-day game at its very best, it would be this one. It was played at the tiny Gymkhana Club in Nairobi during a four-nation tournament in September and October of 1996.

Sri Lanka had won the World Cup earlier in the year, altering the way that ODI cricket was played by attacking the bowling in the first 15 overs. Pakistan were going through one of their periodic rebuilding phases, with the poisoned chalice of captaincy passing this time to opening batsman Saeed Anwar.

South Africa and Kenya were the other two teams in Nairobi, with the former already through to the final when this game was played. Sri Lanka were so far ahead on run rate in the tournament that they could afford to lose and still qualify, so when they won the toss and put Pakistan in to bat they were almost halfway into the final.

But beware the caged tiger! With nothing to lose, Anwar and Saleem Elahi put on 60 for the first wicket. Kumara Dharmasena dismissed Elahi for 23 and on to the field walked sixteen-year-old Shahid Afridi for his first ODI innings. Afridi had been flown in from Pakistan's Under-19 tour of the West Indies as a replacement for the injured leg spinner Mushtaq Ahmed. He was quicker through the air than Mushtaq with a particularly devastating 'flipper', but it was his batting in the nets that caught the eyes of the senior players.

Promoted to pinch hit at number three, Afridi proceeded to score the fastest ODI century of all time off just 37 balls. Along the way he hit six fours and an incredible 11 sixes, making 102 of the 126 runs added for the second wicket. The stand lasted just 61 balls and ended when Afridi was caught in the deep with the score at 186 for two. At which point Anwar took over, made his ninth ODI century and spearheaded the drive towards 371 for nine.

That meant that Sri Lanka could afford to lose, but had to get 290 to qualify for the final. They were 27 for four when Arjuna Ranatunga joined Aravinda de Silva. The two heroes of the World Cup final made 122 and 52 respectively, then Dharmasena hit a rapid half-century and at the beginning of the final over the last pair needed 11 off the bowling of Waqar Younis.

Chaminda Vaas hit Younis' first ball for six, followed it up with another boundary and, with two balls remaining and one run needed, was bowled by a trademark Yorker for 16. Pakistan had won by 82 runs in all, but in the match within a match they reached the final by one run with one ball to spare. In a batsman's match, off-spinner Saqlain Mushtaq took four for 33, somewhat better figures than Sanath Jayasuriya's three for 94!

KCA Centenary Tournament, 1996/97
Pakistan v Sri Lanka
Gymkhana Club Ground, Nairobi
4 October 1996 (50-overs match)

Result: Pakistan won by 82 runs

Pakistan innings
*Saeed Anwar c Mahanama b Muralitharan 115
Saleem Elahi c Muralitharan b Dharmasena 23
Shahid Afridi c Murali'ran b KS de Silva 102
Rameez Raja c Gurusinha b Muralitharan 7
Salim Malik c Ranatunga b PA de Silva 43
Ijaz Ahmed st Kaluwitharana b Jayasuriya 6
+Moin Khan c Dharmasena b Jayasuriya 18
Waqar Younis c Dharmasena b Jayasuriya 12
Azhar Mahmood run out (Dharmasena) 0
Saqlain Mushtaq not out 13
Shahid Nazir not out 6
Extras (lb 7, w 17, nb 2) 26
Total (9 wickets, 50 overs) 371

FoW: 1-60 (Salim Elahi), 2-186 (Shahid Afridi), 3-207 (Rameez Raja), 4-299 (Saeed Anwar), 5-314 (Ijaz Ahmed), 6-322 (Salim Malik), 7-335 (Waqar Younis), 8-336 (Azhar Mahmood), 9-364 (Moin Khan).

Bowling	O	M	R	W
KSC de Silva	6	0	47	1
Vaas	7	0	44	0
Dharmasena	7	0	48	1
Jayasuriya	10	0	94	3
Muralitharan	10	0	73	2
PA de Silva	10	0	58	1

Sri Lanka innings
ST Jayasuriya c Shahid Nazir b Waqar Younis 2
+RS Kaluwitharana c Moin Khan b Waqar Younis .19
AP Gurusinha b Waqar Younis 1
PA de Silva st Moin Khan b Saqlain Mushtaq 122
RS Mahanama lbw b Waqar Younis 0
*A Ranatunga c Moin Khan b Shahid Afridi 52
HP Tillakaratne b Saqlain Mushtaq 3
HDPK Dharmasena c Saeed Anwar b Saqlain Mushtaq 51
WPUJC Vaas b Waqar Younis 16
M Muralitharan st Moin Khan b Saqlain Mushtaq 0
KSC de Silva not out 0
Extras (lb 10, w 12, nb 1) 23
Total (all out, 49.5 overs) 289

FoW: 1-4 (Jayasuriya), 2-26 (Kaluwitharana), 3-27 (Gurusinha), 4-27 (Mahanama), 5-151 (Ranatunga), 6-160 (Tillakaratne), 7-270 (PA de Silva), 8-279 (Dharmasena), 9-279 (Muralitharan), 10-289 (Vaas).

Bowling	O	M	R	W
Waqar Younis	8.5	0	52	5
Azhar Mahmood	5	2	39	0
Shahid Nazir	2	0	32	0
Saqlain Mushtaq	10	2	33	4
Salim Malik	10	0	58	0
Shahid Afridi	10	0	43	1
Saeed Anwar	1	0	8	0
Ijaz Ahmed	3	0	14	0

Hansie Cronjé remembers Afridi's innings distinctly. 'I was commentating on the match because we had a couple of days off. The Gymkhana Club is a relatively small ground, but the sixes Afridi hit weren't sixes, they were twelves. They went over the car park, over the scoreboard, over the commentary box.

'It was more devastating than Adrian Kuiper's century in Bloemfontein because it came up front against the new ball, whereas Kuiper's came in the middle of the innings. He also hit slow bowlers as well as quicks, which was not really the case in Kuiper's innings.

'What made it so remarkable was that nobody was expecting him to walk to the crease. He was sixteen years old, in the side for his leg-spin bowling and had to borrow pads and a bat from other members of the team! He just went berserk, but it was still slightly unreal because you just thought that, OK he'll hit a few sixes, but then he'll pop one up, but he never did.'

While researching this book I discovered another remarkable aspect of this game: the television coverage. We have become accustomed to seeing perfect visuals from wherever cricket is played in the world, with run-outs from half a dozen angles, super slow-mo close-ups of the ball and graphics that describe every conceivable situation. But when the game is played away from regular venues there is always an aspect of making it up as you go along and Nairobi in 1996 was a typical example.

I spoke to well-known South African cameraman Wain Stanton about this match. Wain is in demand all over the world for his camera work, especially on cricket, and has seen it all. He takes up the story.

'It was a very strange day indeed. The crew was all South African, directed by Richard Parker, and we had to cover this one-day series at two venues in Nairobi with a couple of tons of equipment that had to be set up and packed away every time we had to move venues, once with only the evening separating the two games.

'A local farmer lent us his horse truck so that we could build a semi-permanent production vehicle to make the trip between venues easier. It was understandably a little smelly at first, but well worth it if you had to consider the amount of time it saved.

'We had ten cameras that day and about an hour before Afridi walked on everything went bang and we ended up with only three. I was on "ball-follow" at one end, Douglas was at midwicket and Ross on one of the ground cameras. Now it's bad enough when more than half of your equipment has gone down and all you can hear are people desperately trying to rectify the situation and the director trying to do the best with what he's got, but then a batsman walks on to the park that no one has ever heard of and goes and hits a hundred off 37 balls!

'There's a saying, "lights, cameras, chaos!" and that was just such a day! Eventually we opened our two-way communications to the director with the idea that if you think you have the ball then shout your number and the director would cut to you and hopefully you would have the ball in frame. Most of the times we thought and even prayed that we had the ball so that the production could look a little better, but we never had a chance!

'Afridi was hitting the ball so cleanly and so hard that it was going way over our heads. Once Douglas shouted, "I've got it", Richard cut to him and he followed the ball out of the park. But just at that moment when you expect the ball to fall to earth it went up instead of down! He had been following a pigeon!

'I think that was the only ball that Afridi mishit and it actually landed on the oval! Needless to say when he was eventually out we all breathed a sigh of relief, but discussed his innings at length after the game. We were all quite happy to have been there, especially those whose cameras weren't working who could enjoy the innings without trying to follow anything and everything that moved in that big, blue sky.'

Shahid Afridi was just 16 years old when he scored the fastest century yet recorded in ODI cricket, off 37 balls. To make it even more remarkable it was on debut with borrowed kit.
(Getty Images/Touchline Photo)

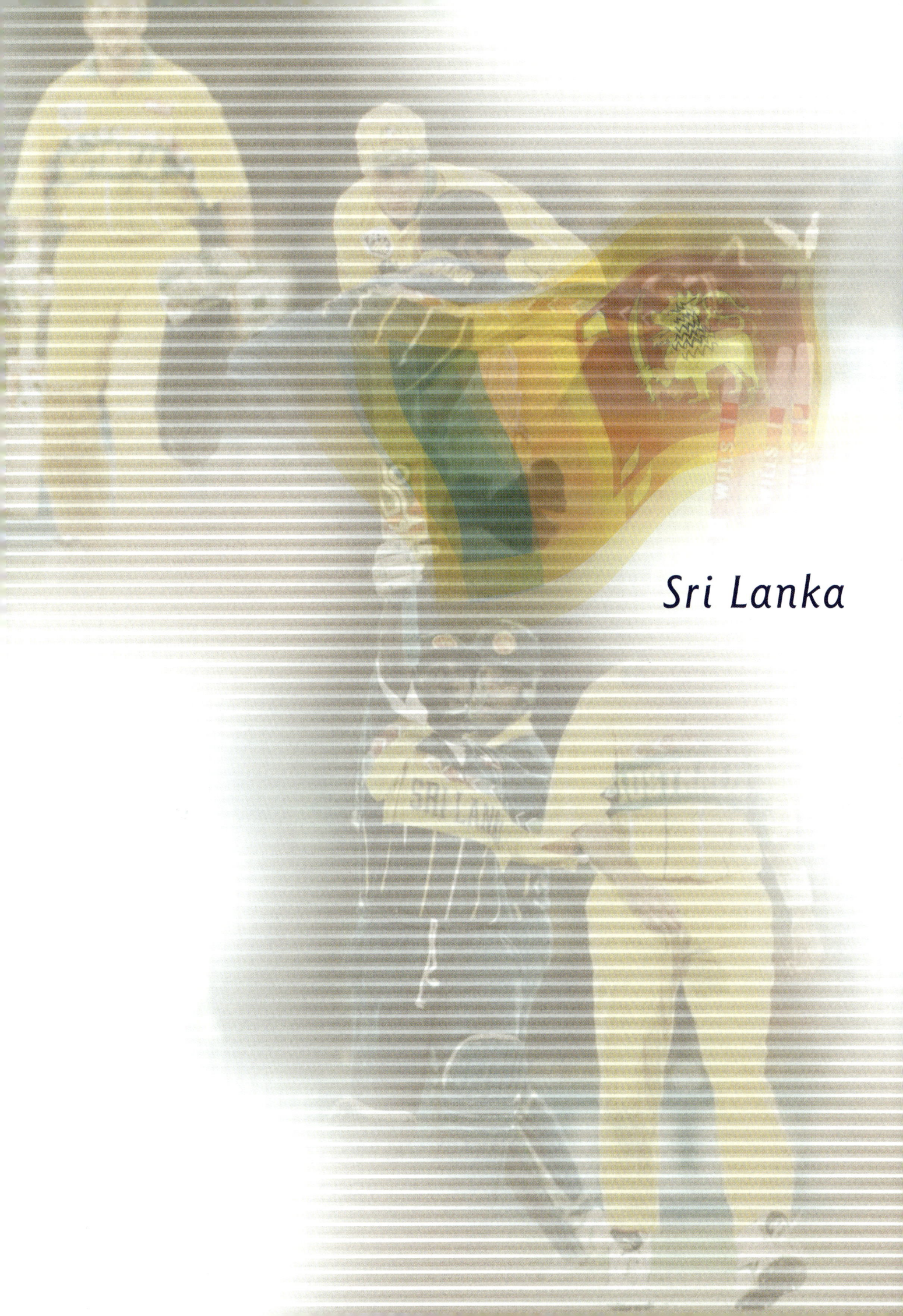

Sri Lanka

Of few teams in the history of sport can it be said that they changed the way the game is played, but that was Sri Lanka's achievement at the 1996 World Cup. Ignoring the accepted dictum that wickets in hand are worth more than a healthy run rate, Sri Lanka dominated the tournament by attacking for all they were worth in the first 15 overs, when only two fielders were allowed outside the 30-metre circle.

Sixty or 70 off the first 15 with no more than one wicket down had been considered the perfect start hitherto, but during the World Cup Sanath Jayasuriya and Romesh Kaluwitharana ensured 15-over starts for their team of 90, 117 (of which 42 came in the first three overs), 123 and 121. In the quarter-final against India, Jayasuriya and Kaluwitharana were both out in the first over and Asanka Gurusinha soon followed. Aravinda de Silva came in and when he got out in the 15th over he had made 66 off 47 balls and the score was 85 for four, a position from which Sri Lanka made 251 for five. In the final the openers again failed, and from 23 for two De Silva's masterly century took them to victory with almost four overs to spare.

This was cricket of a kind that had not been seen before. Searching for a description of the early carnage the press came up with 'pinch hitting' a term borrowed from baseball. It didn't really describe what was happening, but no one found a better way and the term has been used in cricket ever since.

Several things conspired to create Sri Lanka's tactic. The refinement of the 30-metre circle rule demanded two close catchers and no more than two boundary fielders in the first 15 overs. The tournament was played in Asia on wickets devoid of seam movement, but receptive to spin, which meant that the best time to attack the bowling was early, when the faster bowlers were on. And as important as anything else was the appointment of Dav Whatmore as Sri Lanka's coach and master tactician.

Whatmore was Sri Lankan born, but he grew up in Australia and played seven Test matches for his adopted country in the late 1970s. He thus understood both the psyche of cricketers from his native land and the hard-edged spirit in which the game was played in Australia. He also understood that success in one-day cricket could have a positive spin-off in the Test arena, and so it proved.

This is the kind of picture that gets Muttiah Muralitharan into trouble. The master off-spinner has been accused of chucking more than once in his career, but has finally satisfied the critics, allowing him to lead the Sri Lankan attack for the foreseeable future.
(Getty Images/Touchline Photo)

Muttiah Muralitharan is classified as a finger spinner, but this photograph in the moment before delivery shows that he is really a wrist spinner, and a damn fine one at that.
(Getty Images/Touchline Photo)

Until Sanath Jayasuriya was pushed up to open the innings he was used more as a slow left-arm bowler who could bat at seven or eight in ODIs. He has retained his ability to take important wickets and with his low, spearing flight, is very difficult to get away.
(Getty Images/Touchline Photo)

Jayasuriya had been a lower middle-order batsman who bowled flat left-arm spin for the national side for five years before the 1996 World Cup. He was averaging just 34 with the bat and seemed to have a particular dislike of fast bowling. Whatmore pushed him up to open the batting, gave him carte blanche to play his shots and the rest is history. It is quite possible that without Whatmore's hunch Jayasuriya would have drifted out of Test cricket well before he had a chance to score a triple century against India in Colombo in 1999.

In retrospect, it is easy to see why Sri Lanka made the breakthrough in ODIs before they did in Test matches. In common with the rest of the Associate Members of the ICC, the only domestic cricket played on the island had been of the one-day variety. Indeed, what marked the early years of Sri Lanka's campaign for Test status was the ability of their bowlers to play some vivid strokes with the bat. This was because they understood the need to always keep the scoreboard ticking over and early in their Test career Sri Lanka actually made 350 in a Test innings where the whole side made 30s and no one reached 50.

The need to be able to contribute with both bat and ball meant that Sri Lanka always had plenty of allrounders, from the early pioneers such as D S de Silva and Ravi Ratnayeke, through to the stars of the 1996 World Cup, Jayasuriya and Aravinda de Silva, both of whom contributed massively with the ball in addition to their prodigious feats with the bat.

Sri Lanka had been playing Test cricket for fourteen years when the tournament came along that would change their cricket and the world game for ever. The 1996 World Cup gave Sri Lanka much more than a trophy: it gave them self-respect. They have not looked back since.

De Silva Wins Gold

Great moments inspire great players to achieve great things. The sixth World Cup final featured the finest innings yet played in the concluding match of the competition. Aravinda de Silva's 107 not out was not as violent as Clive Lloyd's 102 off 85 balls in 1975, nor as stubborn as Viv Richards' 138 not out in 1979. It was, instead, the most calculated piece of batting that has ever graced a one-day arena.

When De Silva came in Sri Lanka were 23 for two with Sanath Jayasuriya (the player of the tournament) and Romesh Kaluwitharana, the pair who had ensured great starts for the team throughout the tournament, back in the pavilion. De Silva had to start the innings from scratch. He got great support from Asanka Gurusinha and Arjuna Ranatunga, but Sri Lanka won with ease because De Silva batted through the innings to make 107 not out off 124 balls. There was no assault and battery and no panic. Sri Lanka became the first team to win the World Cup final batting second and they won by a record seven-wicket margin with 22 balls to spare.

This was the first game under lights ever played in Pakistan and Dav Whatmore made sure that his team would be prepared by

Aravinda de Silva reaches his century in the 1996 World Cup final. It was the third century in a World Cup final, not as brutal as Clive Lloyd's in 1975 or as inevitable as Viv Richards' in 1979, but aesthetically probably the best of the lot.
(Getty Images/Touchline Photo)

making them practise in the evenings the week prior to the match. Sri Lanka soon discovered that heavy dew was a huge factor and that the team fielding second was at a distinct disadvantage. Bob Simpson, the Australian coach, made his team practise during the day and so did not discover the downside of fielding second until it was too late. Accordingly, when Ranatunga won the toss in the final, Australia were happy to be put in to bat: they would have batted first anyway.

Their captain Mark Taylor played one of his finest one-day innings to set up a powerful position. He made 74 with eight fours and a six and when he was out, sweeping De Silva to deep backward square, Australia were 137 for two in the 27th over. It was a position from which they would have expected to score at least 270, perhaps even 300. Instead, Ranatunga brought back his best bowler, Muttiah Muralitharan and the life was slowly strangled from the innings. Between the 20th and 40th overs Australia scored just 68 runs for the loss of four wickets. Taylor hit nine boundaries, his teammates managed five between them and 241 seemed well short of a good score.

In the quarter-final against England, Jayasuriya had all but won the game in the first 15 overs. Chasing 235 to win, Jayasuriya was out in the 13th over, having made 82 from 44 balls. The scoreboard read 113 for two, almost halfway there with 37 overs left. In the final, Kaluwitharana went early, pulling Damien Fleming to Michael Bevan at square leg, and then Jayasuriya was run out by millimetres: it took several views of the incident for the TV umpire to make the decision and there were plenty of people who believed that he got it wrong. But perhaps if he had got it right we would never have had the chance to savour the innings of a lifetime.

De Silva hit the first ball he received back past the bowler with a model on-drive for three, then whipped Fleming through square leg for four and, far from being filled with nervous tension, his innings gained a momentum that it never lost. Australia made mistakes in the field: Stuart Law dropped Gurusinha at deep square leg when he had made 53 and three half-chances were not taken. Ranatunga had four spinners to call on and when the seamers had gone for 72 in the first 13 overs of the innings they were never seen again. By contrast, Taylor had only two spinners, Shane Warne, the master leg-spinner, and Mark Waugh, an occasional bowler of off-spin, and both discovered to their chagrin that in the wet conditions they could not grip the ball.

Gurusinha began slowly, but flat batted Warne for four over long-off and for six over long-on from successive balls and might have gone all the way had it not been for a wild swing against Paul Reiffel when he had made 65 from 99 balls. He and De Silva had added 125 for the third wicket, but the job was not yet done. Any Australian hopes of a further breakthrough were dashed, however, as Sri Lanka's captain and most experienced cricketer came to the crease. Ranatunga hit his first ball for four on his way to 47 from 37 balls. Those statistics suggest that he blasted away throughout, but in

---

Wills World Cup, 1996, Final
Australia v Sri Lanka
Gaddafi Stadium, Lahore (day/night)
17 March 1996 (50-overs match)

Result: Sri Lanka won by 7 wickets
Sri Lanka wins the 1995/96 Wills World Cup

Australia innings
*MA Taylor c Jayasuriya b de Silva 74
ME Waugh c Jayasuriya b Vaas..............................12
RT Ponting b de Silva 45
SR Waugh c de Silva b Dharmasena 13
SK Warne st Kaluwitharana b Muralitharan 2
SG Law c de Silva b Jayasuriya 22
MG Bevan not out 36
+IA Healy b de Silva 2
PR Reiffel not out 13
Extras (lb 10, w 11, nb 1) 22
Total (7 wickets, 50 overs) 241

DNB: DW Fleming, GD McGrath.

FoW: 1-36 (ME Waugh), 2-137 (Taylor), 3-152 (Ponting), 4-156 (Warne), 5-170 (SR Waugh), 6-202 (Law), 7-205 (Healy).

Bowling	O	M	R	W
Wickramasinghe	7	0	38	0
Vaas	6	1	30	1
Muralitharan	1	0	31	1
Dharmasena	1	0	47	1
Jayasuriya	8	0	43	1
de Silva	9	0	42	3

Sri Lanka innings
ST Jayasuriya run out 9
+RS Kaluwitharana c Bevan b Fleming 6
AP Gurusinha b Reiffel 65
PA de Silva not out 107
*A Ranatunga not out 47
Extras (b 1, lb 4, w 5, nb 1) 11
Total (3 wickets, 46.2 overs) 245

DNB: HP Tillakaratne, RS Mahanama, HDPK Dharmasena, WPUJC Vaas, GP Wickramasinghe, M Muralitharan.

FoW: 1-12 (Jayasuriya), 2-23 (Kaluwitharana), 3-148 (Gurusinha).

Bowling	O	M	R	W
McGrath	8.2	1	28	0
Fleming	6	0	43	1
Warne	10	0	58	0
Reiffel	10	0	49	1
ME Waugh	6	0	35	0
SR Waugh	3	0	15	0
Bevan	3	0	12	0

Arjuna Ranatunga starts the party. The Sri Lankan captain had scarcely tickled the ball away for the winning run in the 1996 World Cup final when he was engulfed by team mates who had raced across the field. From the left: Upal Chandana, Pramodya Wickramasinghe, Aravinda de Silva, Ranatunga, Ravindra Pushpakumara, and Kumar Dharmasena. The distraught Australians are Shane Warne and Paul Reiffel, both of whom would have to wait for the next World Cup to understand the emotions of the Sri Lankan players. Interestingly, in the hunt for souvenirs, Wickramasinghe seems to have settled on the stump microphone.
(Getty Images/Touchline Photo)

fact, after that first ball boundary, he spent time playing himself in and when the last 10 overs began there were still 51 runs needed. Then the pyrotechnics started, the pair scored at eight an over until the 45th when, with boundaries having become unnecessary, they stroked their way to victory in ones and twos.

It was fitting that these two were there to finish the match. They had both captained the team and were by some distance its best players. De Silva was a classic player, immensely strong off the back foot with wrists of such strength that he could hit a straight ball almost anywhere on the on-side. For a year either side of this match a good claim could be made for him, and not Brian Lara or Sachin Tendulkar, to be the best batsman in the world. He had all the shots and a temperament to match, but this game was unquestionably his finest moment.

'The image will long remain,' wrote Christopher Martin-Jenkins in the Telegraph, 'one of the most romantic in the continuously evolving history of cricket. Half past ten on a misty night in Lahore as the rain begins to fall. Arjuna Ranatunga, a tubby little 32-year-old in dark blue shirt and trousers, holds up a huge silver trophy: a monument to a little nation's marvellous sporting achievement.'
(Getty Images/Touchline Photo)

A poignant moment. Arjuna Ranatunga hugs Aravinda de Silva as the latter completes his match-winning century in the 1996 World Cup final.
(Getty Images/Touchline Photo)

Sanath Jayasuriya celebrates taking the wicket of Australia's Stuart Law in the 1996 World Cup final. Aravinda de Silva, who offers Jayasuriya a high ten, caught Law close in. Romesh Kaluwitharana is between them, Roshan Mahanama in the background.
(Getty Images/Touchline Photo)

Ranatunga, in addition to being left-handed, was De Silva's opposite in most other respects. He seldom came forward and scored most of his runs behind square with deflections rather than hits. His secret was that he played every ball under his nose, almost suicidally late. He frequently appeared to cut the ball from out of the wicketkeeper's gloves and many an lbw appeal was strangled at birth as the bat came down to deflect the ball past despairing fielders. De Silva's innings won the match, but Ranatunga hit the winning run, a trademark deflection to third man.

Twinkle toes. Sri Lankan wicketkeeper Romesh Kaluwitharana flicks off the bails, but Michael Bevan is safe. Bevan ended 36 not out as Australia made 241 for seven. Stuart Law is at the non-striker's end.
(Getty Images/Touchline Photo)

There were those who tried to argue that a bomb blast in Colombo two weeks prior to the tournament had been too influential: both Australia and the West Indies forfeited their matches against Sri Lanka because they would not travel to Colombo. But it is difficult to believe that things would have turned out differently if those games had been played. This was quite simply Sri Lanka's moment in history and nothing, not bomb blasts in their capital or crowd invasions in Calcutta, could defeat an idea whose time had come.

Aravinda de Silva cuts on the way to his match-winning century against Australia in the 1996 World Cup final. De Silva is a great cutter and puller, like many small men. Notice here the perfect balance and how the wrists have rolled so the ball goes down, not up. Wicketkeeper Ian Healy is lost in admiration.
(Getty Images/Touchline Photo)

Sanath Jayasuriya was voted the player of the 1996 World Cup the day before the final against Australia at the Gaddafi Stadium in Lahore. But he failed with the bat in the final and was run out for 9, a fact celebrated by Damien Fleming in the background as wicketkeeper Ian Healy removes the bails.
(Getty Images/Touchline Photo)

The Volcano Erupts

Just two weeks after their glorious World Cup triumph Sri Lanka were playing ODIs again, this time for the Singer Trophy against India and Pakistan in the unlikely venue of Singapore. Although Sanath Jayasuriya had won the man of the tournament award at the World Cup he had failed to post a century, his highest score being 82. Against Pakistan at the tiny Padang ground in Singapore, he made up for that omission with the fastest century in ODI history, a mark that, remarkably, stood for only a year before being beaten by Shahid Afridi in another match between the two Asian rivals at another small ground, this time in Nairobi.

It was an innings filled with records and it came on the second day of a match restarted after rain on the previous day. Jayasuriya's knock eclipsed Mohammad Azharuddin's previous record of 62 balls. He reached three figures in 48 balls and in all made 134 off 65 balls, 22 of which he propelled to the boundary. His tally of 11 sixes beat Gordon Greenidge's previous ODI record of eight and along the way he made life a misery for Aamer Sohail who set

Sanath Jayasuriya in untypical mood, guiding the ball rather than thrashing it.
(Getty Images/Touchline Photo)

Singer Cup, 1996
Pakistan v Sri Lanka
The Padang, Singapore
2 April 1996 (50-overs match)

Result: Sri Lanka won by 34 runs

Sri Lanka innings

ST Jayasuriya c M Akram b S Mushtaq	134
+RS Kaluwitharana c Saqlain Mushtaq b Waqar Younis	24
AP Gurusinha c Aamer Sohail b Saqlain Mushtaq	29
PA de Silva c & b Salim Malik	7
*A Ranatunga c Inzamam-ul-Haq b Waqar Younis	14
HP Tillakaratne b Mohammad Akram	25
RS Mahanama c Waqar Younis b Mohammad Akram	35
HDPK Dharmasena b Waqar Younis	51
WPUJC Vaas c Aamer Sohail b Waqar Younis	6
GP Wickramasinghe not out	7
M Muralitharan not out	2
Extras (b 1, lb 3, w 9, nb 2)	15
Total (9 wickets, 50 overs)	**349**

FoW: 1-40 (Kaluwitharana), 2-196 (Gurusinha), 3-197 (Jayasuriya), 4-203 (de Silva), 5-238 (Ranatunga), 6-245 (Tillakaratne), 7-318 (Mahanama), 8-328 (Vaas), 9-346 (Dharmasena).

Bowling	O	M	R	W
Waqar Younis	10	0	62	4
Mohammad Akram	7	0	66	2
Saqlain Mushtaq	10	0	45	2
Aaqib Javed	10	0	65	0
Aamer Sohail	8	0	73	0
Salim Malik	5	0	34	1

Pakistan innings

*Aamer Sohail lbw b Dharmasena	46
Saeed Anwar c Kaluwitharana b Vaas	32
Rameez Raja c & b de Silva	27
Saleem Malik c Dharmasena b Muralitharan	68
Inzamam-ul-Haq b Vaas	67
Ijaz Ahmed st Kaluwitharana b Jayasuriya	32
Waqar Younis c Muralitharan b Dharmasena	1
+Rashid Latif c Dharmasena b Muralitharan	7
Saqlain Mushtaq run out	0
Aaqib Javed c Muralitharan b Tillakaratne	20
Mohammad Akram not out	3
Extras (b 3, lb 6, w 1, nb 2)	12
Total (all out, 49.4 overs)	**315**

FoW: 1-77 (Saeed Anwar), 2-96 (Aamer Sohail), 3-120 (Rameez Raja), 4-247 (Inzamam-ul-Haq), 5-253 (Salim Malik), 6-257 (Waqar Younis), 7-281 (Rashid Latif), 8-291 (Saqlain Mushtaq), 9-291 (Ijaz Ahmed), 10-315 (Aaqib Javed).

Bowling	O	M	R	W
Wickramasinghe	5	0	46	0
Vaas	10	0	50	2
Muralitharan	10	0	59	2
Dharmasena	8	0	51	2
de Silva	4	0	22	1
Jayasuriya	10	0	45	1
Ranatunga	2	0	20	0
Tillakaratne	0.4	0	13	1

Sanath Jayasuriya is a merciless punisher of the short ball, especially early in the innings when only two boundary fielders are allowed. Note how low down the bat handle he grips and how well balanced he is as he watches the ball race for four.
(Getty Images/Touchline Photo)

another world record, this time for the most runs conceded in a single ODI over. There were 30 in all: Jayasuriya scored 29 and there was one wide.

Jayasuriya's opening partner, Romesh Kaluwitharana actually outscored him during a stand of 40. Kalu' faced only 10 balls before holing out, but he hit two of them for four and two for six, ending on 24. But Jayasuriya was utterly dominant in a second-wicket stand worth 156. He farmed the strike and overwhelmed his partner Asanka Gurusinha so much that the portly left-hander could only manage 29 off 56 balls. To put that in perspective, by the time Jayasuriya had faced 56 balls he had made 120.

Against Kenya at the World Cup, Sri Lanka had scored a world record ODI total of 398 for five. In Singapore they fell short of that mark with a total of 349 for nine, but in reply Pakistan made 315 to contribute to the highest match aggregate in ODIs with a grand total of 664 runs for 19 wickets in 99.4 overs.

Jayasuriya's form continued long enough to convince the world that he was no flash in the pan and, when Ranatunga retired, he was made national captain. At the 1999 World Cup he was less of a factor on the softer English pitches, but while his ODI contributions returned to mere mortal status he began to fulfil his talent in the Test arena. He remains an influential player wherever he goes and there are still days when the magic descends upon him once more and then it is worth a day's walk to watch him bat.

Kenya

Cricket has been played in Kenya for more than a hundred years. In the early twentieth century matches were separately organised by the Asian Sports Association (founded in 1912) and the Kenya Kongonis Cricket Club (founded 1927), the latter looking after the interests of whites. In 1953 the two bodies merged to become the Kenya Cricket Association, the first interracial organisation of its type in the country's history.

Kenya provided seven of the fourteen-man squad that travelled to the first World Cup in 1975 under the banner of East Africa. Among their number was Don Pringle, the father of England allrounder Derek, who played in the 1992 World Cup. Eventually Kenya separated from East Africa and in 1981 was given associate membership of the ICC in its own right.

The breakthrough came towards the end of the 1980s when indigenous Kenyans of African descent began to take an interest in the game. Two families in particular raised the overall standard of cricket in Kenya: the Tikolos and the Odumbes. At the 1982 ICC Trophy the entire Kenyan squad was of Asian descent, but by 1986 Tom Tikolo was the captain of a squad that included Thomas Odumbe and Alfred Njuguna.

By 1990 Tom Tikolo's younger brother David had joined the squad, together with Maurice Odumbe and his cousin Edward Tito Odumbe, and when the ICC Trophy was held in Nairobi in 1994 there were more Africans than Asians in the squad. What made the team so hard to beat, however, was that the issue of race had all but disappeared; this was not a team of transient workers or displaced peoples, it was a team of Kenyans.

In Nairobi they lost in the final to a team who represented all that Kenya had left behind. The United Arab Emirates squad consisted almost entirely of Pakistanis, Indians and Sri Lankans who were economic refugees in the UAE. As such, they should have been subject to rigorous eligibility requirements, but suspicions were raised before the tournament began when it transpired that all fifteen UAE players had the same date stamp on their passport, December 1989. The ICC required a player to have resided in the country for at least four years before representing the national side, so it seemed somewhat odd that all fifteen had been resident in the UAE for exactly four years and two months.

The 1994 tournament was a swansong for Tom Tikolo, who was approaching forty years of age at the time, but it was the launching pad for his youngest brother, the most beguilingly gifted Kenyan cricketer to date, Steve Tikolo. Here was a player who had that indefinable presence at the crease. As we sat and watched Tikolo blaze away at Nairobi Gymkhana one day, Simon Hughes, the former Middlesex and Durham medium pacer who was covering the tournament for the Daily Telegraph, nodded approvingly and said, 'There's a touch of Viv Richards about this fellow.' Eighteen months later Tikolo was part of the Kenyan team that made everyone sit up and take notice at the 1996 World Cup.

Right: *Rajab Ali is surrounded by his team mates after making an early breakthrough against the West Indies in the 1996 World Cup.*
(Getty Images/Touchline Photo)

Kenyan Carnival

For those of us lucky enough to have been in Nairobi for the 1994 ICC Trophy, this was a result that confirmed what we knew. For everyone else it was, and remains, the biggest upset in World Cup history. For Kenya's captain, Maurice Odumbe, it was 'like winning the World Cup. It's a dream come true. The West Indies are our idols, and to beat an idol is a great thing. We came to the World Cup with a promise that we could play. I think we proved it today.'

They proved it in emphatic style. This was not an edge-of-the-seat nail-biter; it was a good, old-fashioned thumping. Put in to bat, Kenya were bowled out for 166 and responded by dismissing the Windies for 93, the second lowest score in their history, giving the underdogs victory by 73 runs. They may have been a shadow of the side that won the first two World Cups, but this was still a proud Windies side as evinced by the reaction of their captain, Richie Richardson, after the game.

Richardson said, 'My congratulations to Kenya for winning a very important match. We did not play the way we should have. I am very, very disappointed. I have nothing more to add.' Then he walked out of the press conference.

Richardson had every reason to be disappointed: the result meant that there was a very real chance the Windies would not progress to the latter stages of the competition. Indeed, it gave Kenya an outside chance of reaching the quarter-finals themselves.

What grass there was on the pitch had a tinge of green, and Kenya's fate seemed sealed when Courtney Walsh struck twice in his first two overs. An edge by Deepak Chudasama escaped the grasp of Roger Harper at second slip, but the rebound stayed in the air long enough for Brian Lara, at first slip, to complete the catch. Walsh then induced a fatal snick from Kennedy Otieno, and Kenya were 19 for two.

Kenya at home were an almost impossibly confident side, but in the big, wide world they were over-reliant on two batsmen, Odumbe and Steve Tikolo. Odumbe failed and so in the normal scheme of things did Tikolo, snicking a catch to the keeper against the off-spin of Harper when the score had reached 77. But in one over Tikolo lofted Walsh to long-off for four and hoisted him for a straight six and as it turned out his 29 off 51 balls was the highest score of the match with the sole exception of extras, which contributed 37 priceless runs to the Kenyan total thanks to the indiscipline of the Windies' bowlers.

Wills World Cup, 1996
Kenya v West Indies,
Nehru Stadium, Poona
29 February 1996 (50-overs match)

Result: Kenya won by 73 runs

Kenya innings

DN Chudasama c Lara b Walsh 8
+IT Iqbal c Cuffy b Walsh 16
KO Otieno c Adams b Walsh 2
SO Tikolo c Adams b Harper 29
*MO Odumbe hit wicket b Bishop 6
HS Modi c Adams b Ambrose 26
MA Suji c Lara b Harper 0
TM Odoyo st Adams b Harper 24
EO Odumbe b Cuffy 1
AY Karim c Adams b Ambrose 11
RW Ali not out 6
Extras (lb 10, w 14, nb 13) 37
Total (all out, 49.3 overs) 166

FoW: 1-15 (Chudasama), 2-19 (Otieno), 3-45 (Iqbal), 4-72 (MO Odumbe), 5-77 (Tikolo), 6-81 (Suji), 7-125 (Odoyo), 8-126 (EO Odumbe), 9-155 (Modi), 10-166 (Karim).

Bowling	O	M	R	W
Ambrose	8.3	1	21	2
Walsh	9	0	46	3
Bishop	10	2	30	1
Cuffy	8	0	31	1
Harper	10	4	15	3
Arthurton	4	0	13	0

West Indies innings

SL Campbell b Suji 4
*RB Richardson b Ali 5
BC Lara c Iqbal b Ali 8
S Chanderpaul c Tikolo b MO Odumbe 19
KLT Arthurton run out 0
+JC Adams c Modi b MO Odumbe 9
RA Harper c Iqbal b MO Odumbe 7
IR Bishop not out 6
CEL Ambrose run out 3
CA Walsh c Chudasama b Karim 4
CE Cuffy b Ali 1
Extras (b 5, lb 6, w 4, nb 2) 17
Total (all out, 35.2 overs) 93

FoW: 1-18 (Richardson), 2-22 (Campbell), 3-33 (Lara), 4-35 (Arthurton), 5-55 (Chanderpaul), 6-65 (Adams), 7-78 (Harper), 8-81 (Ambrose), 9-89 (Walsh), 10-93 (Cuffy).

Bowling	O	M	R	W
Suji	7	2	16	1
Ali	7.2	2	17	3
Karim	8	1	19	1
MO Odumbe	10	3	15	3
Odoyo	3	0	15	0

The elegant left-hander Hitesh Modi made a composed 26 and the allrounder Thomas Odoyo a more rumbustious 24, and the last two wickets added 40 runs, but the Windies bowlers assumed, as they had at the 1983 final, that they had done enough to win the game. They had reckoned without Kenya's remarkable team spirit. They bowled and fielded as if their lives depended on it and at no stage of the Windies innings did it appear likely that Kenya would release their vice-like grip. Wickets fell early and continued to fall at regular intervals until the end.

The first wicket was the result of an in-swinger from Rajab Ali, which defeated Richardson's lavish drive and flattened his off stump. Then Martin Suji bowled Sherwin Campbell behind his legs and Ali dealt the mortal blow when Brian Lara sliced a drive to be caught in the slips by Tariq Iqbal for eight. The West Indies were 33 for three, and two runs later Keith Arthurton was run out, 35 for four.

Another West Indies wicket falls and the Kenyan fielders celebrate. Left to right: *Maurice Odumbe, Steve Tikolo and Hitesh Modi.*
(Getty Images/Touchline Photo)

Shivnarine Chanderpaul dug in, and he and Jimmy Adams put together a partnership of 20, not much, but the highest stand of the innings nonetheless. But when Chanderpaul had made 19 from 48 balls Odumbe, bowling off-breaks, got him to mistime a cut. Odumbe also accounted for Adams, caught at silly point, and Harper, who played for non-existent turn and the Kenyan skipper earned the man of the match award for his return of 10-3-15-3. The match was wrapped up with 15 overs to spare and Odumbe led his team on a lap of honour in front of five thousand spectators at the Nehru Stadium.

Kenya has yet to be accorded Test status, but they do have ODI status, a new dispensation brought in by the ICC. They fall into the category once inhabited by New Zealand and Sri Lanka, out of their depth on tour, but a tough nut to crack at home. Both those nations put systematic early failure behind them long ago and, with Tikolo and Odumbe as role models, Kenyan cricket is assured of the bright future deserved by any team that can beat the West Indies on a foreign field.

Kenya's finest player Steve Tikolo, a batsman in the classic mould who can, on his day, destroy any attack.
(Getty Images/Touchline Photo)

New Zealand

In April of 2002 the International Rugby Board (IRB) awarded the 2003 Rugby World Cup to Australia. In New Zealand this went down like a lead balloon. The Kiwis had been expecting to co-host the tournament with Australia, much as they had done with the 1992 Cricket World Cup, but they could not guarantee to fulfil the IRB's requirements and so were unceremoniously removed from the equation. The consequent trans-Tasman Sea mud-slinging became increasingly personal and, inevitably, included a reference to a cricket match that has passed into infamy.

It is twenty-one years since Trevor Chappell rolled a cricket ball down the pitch to Brian McKechnie, but the wounds opened by his action suppurate still. When a Kiwi really wants to insult an Aussie he only has to mention Chappell's name and then it is as if it all happened yesterday.

The eye of the storm. When he had made 58 Greg Chappell was brilliantly caught in the outfield by Martin Snedden. Lance Cairns, the bowler, described it as, 'The most brilliant catch I've ever seen', but umpire Peter Cronin was not certain it had been taken cleanly and ruled Chappell not out. That was just the start of a bad day for the Australian captain.
(Getty Images/Touchline Photo)

It was the first season after Kerry Packer's World Series Cricket had broken up and the Australian team was an uncomfortable amalgam of former rebels and players such as Allan Border who had been fast-tracked into official international cricket during the Packer players' absence. Greg Chappell, the best and most stylish Australian batsman of the 1970s, who was coming towards the end of an illustrious career, captained them.

Chappell had captained the Australians on the Ashes tour to England in 1977 and was regarded as a saint by the establishment for refusing Packer's initial approach. But at the end of the tour he duly signed on the dotted line and the saint became a sinner. Accordingly, when he resumed the captaincy of the official Australian team three years later there were many in his own country with ambivalent attitudes toward him, a fact that became glaringly obvious after this match against New Zealand at the MCG.

The two sides were engaged in a multi-state best of five match marathon final ODI series, which was currently tied at one each. Fifty-three thousand people, then a record for an ODI, paid their money to watch the game and they were rewarded with a contest that, even if it had not ended in acrimony would still have been memorable.

Chappell won the toss and chose to bat first, which in itself was an odd decision given the make-up of his team. He had seven batsmen and a wicketkeeper and just three specialist bowlers, a line-up that these days would suggest a team happier chasing, rather than setting, a target.

Border fell early and Chappell marched out to join the left-handed Graeme Wood. The pair put on 145, but it was not without incident. When he had made 58 Chappell was brilliantly caught in the outfield by Martin Snedden. Lance Cairns, the bowler, described it as 'the most brilliant catch I've ever seen', but umpire Peter Cronin was not certain it had been taken cleanly and ruled Chappell not out.

Mark Burgess, the fielder closest to Snedden, was adamant it was out and a livid Snedden ran in and remonstrated with Chappell, but the Australian captain stood his ground and went on to top score with 90 from 122 balls with seven boundaries. Australia totalled 235 for four from their 50 overs, a good score but not unbeatable in friendly conditions for batting.

New Zealand had two left-handers at the top of the order and they put on 85 in gritty fashion. John Wright and Bruce Edgar saw off the threat of Dennis Lillee and Max Walker with the new ball and Chappell had to bowl his own slow-medium trundlers at an earlier stage than he would have wished. Nevertheless he effected the breakthrough, having Wright caught by Martin Kent for 42.

Edgar was the lynchpin of the innings and his century kept the Kiwis in the hunt despite the regular loss of wickets at the other end.

Benson & Hedges World Series Cup, 1980/81, 3rd Final
Australia v New Zealand
Melbourne Cricket Ground
1 February 1981 (50-overs match)

Result: Australia won by 6 runs

Australia innings
AR Border c Parker b Hadlee 5
GM Wood b McEwan 72
*GS Chappell c Edgar b Snedden 90
MF Kent c Edgar b Snedden 33
+RW Marsh not out 18
KD Walters not out 6
Extras (b 8, lb 3) 11
Total (4 wickets, 50 overs) 235

DNB: KJ Hughes, GR Beard, TM Chappell, DK Lillee, MHN Walker.

FoW: 1-8 (Border), 2-153 (Wood), 3-199 (GS Chappell), 4-215 (Kent).

Bowling	O	M	R	W
Hadlee	10	0	41	1
Snedden	10	0	52	2
Cairns	10	0	34	0
McKechnie	10	0	54	0
McEwan	7	1	31	1
Howarth	3	0	12	0

New Zealand innings
JG Wright c Kent b GS Chappell 42
BA Edgar not out 102
*GP Howarth c Marsh b GS Chappell 18
BL Cairns b Beard 12
MG Burgess c TM Chappell b GS Chappell 2
PE McEwan c Wood b Beard 11
JM Parker c TM Chappell b Lillee 24
RJ Hadlee lbw b TM Chappell 4
+IDS Smith b TM Chappell 4
BJ McKechnie not out 0
Extras (lb 10) 10
Total (8 wickets, 50 overs) 229

DNB: MC Snedden.

FoW: 1-85 (Wright), 2-117 (Howarth), 3-136 (Cairns), 4-139 (Burgess), 5-172 (McEwan), 6-221 (Parker), 7-225 (Hadlee), 8-229 (Smith).

Bowling	O	M	R	W
Lillee	10	1	34	1
Walker	10	0	35	0
Beard	10	0	50	2
GS Chappell	10	0	43	3
TM Chappell	10	0	57	2

He found a good ally in John Parker who lashed 24 off 19 balls in a stand worth 49, but the pair were separated by Lillee in the penultimate over of the match and Edgar lost the strike for the final over, from which 15 were required.

There are those who have suggested that Chappell got his sums wrong and that Lillee should have bowled the last over, not the penultimate one. As it transpired he had no option but to bowl his brother Trevor. Richard Hadlee hit the first ball of the final over for four; now the requirement was 11 off five deliveries. Going for another big hit, Hadlee missed and was lbw to the next. In came wicketkeeper Ian Smith who steered the next two balls for a couple each, seven now needed off two.

Trevor Chappell was the youngest of the three Chappell brothers and lacking in the eye-catching skills of Ian and Greg. He was a middle-order batsman with very few strokes and his brief international career seems to have owed much to the fact that he could bowl respectable medium pace. It is a strange fact that Australia has not produced a world-class allrounder since Keith Miller. Trevor Chappell was scarcely in that class and he was never going to frighten anyone out, but he could bowl line and length and he had a good temperament. But he was, by some way, the weakest of the five bowlers available to Greg and shouldn't have been placed in such an invidious position in the first place.

Trevor Chappell delivers the ball that forever soured relations between Australia and New Zealand.

In the 1992 World Cup New Zealand captain Martin Crowe experimented with the ploy of opening the bowling with pace at one end, spin at the other. Dipak Patel bowled his off-spin with conspicuous success on the slow New Zealand pitches and Crowe's team got all the way to the semi-final. Here Patel is congratulated on taking another wicket by Chris Cairns.
(Getty Images/Touchline Photo)

Yet Trevor rose to the occasion. He bowled straight, pinned Hadlee lbw and with his fifth ball bowled Smith. The Kiwis in the crowd let out sighs of remorse: their team's chance had gone. But Greg Chappell looked at the scoreboard and realised that six off the final ball would tie the game, a result that would ensure the series went to the fifth and final match. It had already been a long and arduous season and there was a Test series yet to be played. Chappell decided he would do anything to avoid having to play that fifth match, so he wandered over to Trevor and said, 'How are you at bowling your underarms?'

Upon that thought Greg Chappell's career was for ever soured. The upright and elegant compiler of Test match centuries, an Australian all-time great, had a moment of madness and there was no one capable of talking him out of it. He had played in a WSC game a couple of years earlier where West Indian quick bowler Wayne Daniel had slogged the final ball of the match for six to win the game and Chappell was determined that history would not repeat itself.

He had seen the imposing form of All Black rugby player Brian McKechnie emerge from the pavilion, swinging his bat in a manner that suggested that he believed a miracle was possible. Chappell knew that a good length ball such as the ones his brother had been propelling hitherto would be in McKechnie's arc and he determined to take the long hit out of the equation.

He ordered Trevor to roll the ball along the ground, and while he afterwards admitted that he might have been on the verge of a nervous breakdown, Greg was in control enough to tell the umpire first, thereby avoiding a no-ball for an unannounced change of action.

Rod Marsh called out from behind the stumps, 'No mate, don't do it', but Trevor said afterwards, 'It didn't enter my mind to say no. I actually didn't consider it to be a yes/no type of question. It was the captain of my team asking me to do something that was, at the time anyway, within the rules of the game. It seemed like a good idea.'

What Trevor did not mention, of course, was that the captain was his elder brother, a man who might not actually be on the selection committee, but who was capable of controlling his future international destiny.

Umpire Cronin consulted with umpire Don Weser at square leg, informed the batsman and the match ended not with a bang, but a whimper. McKechnie, the man who had gone out there for death or glory, defended the ball, threw his bat away and stood in the middle of the pitch glaring at Trevor. If looks could kill . . .

Up to this moment the biggest controversy in ODIs had been Sunil Gavaskar's attempt to play for a draw in the 1975 World Cup. There were still those in authority who believed that one-day cricket would be a short-term fad, but the reaction to the anticlimax of this match proved them spectacularly wrong.

Facing page: *New Zealand's greatest cricketer, Sir Richard Hadlee was a late developer. He began as a wild and woolly fast bowler, but developed into one of the finest allrounders the game has seen. The turning point for Hadlee came when Nottinghamshire tempted him to turn professional and play county cricket in England. Thrown into an environment where he was playing virtually every day, Hadlee decided to shorten his run to the wicket and with greater balance at the crease he became a masterful bowler, able to swing the ball either way at will.*

With the greater control, however, there was scarcely a diminution of pace. He was capable of bowling a mean bouncer and could make the ball spit at the batsman from just short of a length. Hadlee looked after his body so well that he was able to endure in international cricket into middle age and he actually took a wicket with his final ball in Test cricket.
(Getty Images/Touchline Photo)

Richard Hadlee whips another one away. Hadlee's sojourn in county cricket also had the effect of improving his batting. His technique was never perfect, but he had the ability to hit good balls for four, a sure way to upset any bowler. In the notorious match against Australia in 1981, Hadlee took the wicket of Allan Border with the new ball, finishing with one for 41 from his 10 overs. He came in to bat at number nine with New Zealand needing 15 to win and hit the first ball of the final over for four, before falling lbw to Trevor Chappell (bowling overarm at this stage) next ball.
(Getty Images/Touchline Photo)

Richie Benaud, a former captain of Australia who was commentating at the time said: 'You can have your own opinions about that, but let me tell you what mine is. I think it was a gutless performance from the Australian captain.'

New Zealand's Prime Minister Robert Muldoon called it 'The most disgusting incident in the history of cricket. If the bloody Australians want it they'll get it fair between the eyes!'

McKechnie, who never again played for his country, said, 'The chance of my hitting a six must have been one in thousands', but Doug Walters threw down the gauntlet to his fellow Aussies at practice in Sydney a couple of days later. Allan Border had $10 with Walters that he couldn't hit his underarm delivery for six and Rod Marsh acted as referee and stakeholder. Border rolled the ball; Walters flicked it up with his boot and swatted it out of the ground. Trying to save his money Border appealed for lbw; 'Not out,' said Marsh. 'Too far down the wicket.'

Trevor Chappell played on in the national side for a couple more seasons, but had it not been for the underarm delivery at the MCG he would have been largely forgotten. He was invited to play in a double-wicket competition in New Zealand a few years later. His partner was Brian McKechnie.

Mark Greatbatch made a huge impression at the 1992 World Cup, scoring at more than a run a ball at the top of the innings, thrashing the ball over and through the infield in the first 15 overs. New Zealand got good starts in virtually every game, none more so than against South Africa where Greatbatch's frantic 68 urged his side to victory with more than 15 overs to spare. But Ken Rutherford, who batted below Greatbatch in the tournament and later captained New Zealand, remembers how different it might have been for the chunky left-hander.

'He got into our final squad for the '92 World Cup as the last player selected. He had endured a lean time of it, struggling for runs in previous series. Remember this was the same Mark Greatbatch who batted over ten hours at the WACA in 1989, defying Merv Hughes and Craig McDermott to save a Test against Australia.

'Greatbatch only played against South Africa because John Wright pulled out on the morning prior to the match with a hamstring problem. The story goes that our coach Warren Lees spoke to Greatbatch before he went in and suggested he was in such woeful form that he might as well get out there and have a bash. If he tried to hang around and bat properly he'd get out anyway, so may as well get out there, throw the bat, get as many as he could quickly, and get out. Let some other guy have a chance.

'In a way this World Cup hindered his future career. Having shown that he could fling the bat at a merry rate and also hang around in a more dour fashion, in ensuing innings he often got caught between the two styles; but he was a very fine player, who on his day, could turn the course of a match.'
(Getty Images/Touchline Photo)

Bangladesh

In Bangladesh, as in most parts of Asia, cricket matters rather more than Western minds can conceive. For a start it's been played there for nearly two centuries, from the time it was Bengal through the years it spent as East Pakistan (Pakistan played Test matches in Dhaka during the 1950s and 60s) and right up to date. Only one-day cricket was played there until Bangladesh was granted Test status on 26 June 2000. Their inaugural Test match was against India in Dhaka in November 2001.

Mohammad Rafique bowls Waqar Younis to reduce Pakistan to 160 for nine. After a 36-run stand for the ninth wicket between Younis and Saqlain Mushtaq had raised faint hopes of revival, Rafique's breakthrough all but clinched the match with only Shoaib Akhtar to come. The wicketkeeper is Khaled Mashud.
(Getty Images/Touchline Photo)

I never understood what cricket meant to Bangladesh until I went to the ICC Trophy in Nairobi in 1994. Bangladesh lost a preliminary group match against Kenya at the Simba Union ground, a result that ended their hopes of qualifying for the 1996 World Cup in Asia. The press sat with some of the officials in a turret at the top of the main stand and as we hammered away against various deadlines a whirling dervish came flying across our bows.

This, it transpired, was the Bangladeshi assistant manager Golam Faruque Apu and requests for him to 'shut up' were met with wild screams and flying fists. He attacked the table where a commentary team was broadcasting proceedings back to Bangladesh. The correspondent of the local paper nearly had his typewriter hurled from the roof as he sought to confront the man and it finally took several members of his own team to restrain him. 'What,' we asked ourselves, 'was the problem? His team had lost a cricket match, it wasn't the end of the world.'

How naïve we were. A week later it was reported by Reuters that the Bangladesh Cricket Union offices in Dhaka had been burned to the ground by a crazed mob of disappointed cricket fans. Fearing for his life, Apu did not fly home with the rest of the team. I often wonder if he ever made it. Five years later, Bangladesh finally made it to the World Cup proper and while they generally failed to play to their potential, they produced one result that will be talked about as long as cricket is played.

Saqlain Mushtaq is run out to end the match and all hell breaks loose. The pitch invasion was a touch premature as the decision was referred to the third umpire, but fortunately for the participants it favoured Bangladesh and the ground did not have to be cleared to restart the game.

(Getty Images/Touchline Photo)

Bangladesh's Moment in the Sun

While this result did not register quite as high on the Richter Scale as Kenya's defeat of the West Indies in 1996, in retrospect it took on far greater importance. During a commission of inquiry into the match fixing scandals brought about by the resignation of Hansie Cronjé, it was cited by Ali Bacher, managing director of the United Cricket Board of South Africa (UCBSA), as a suspicious result.

Twelve months down the line Bacher was merely reiterating what had been said at the time. Pakistan captain Wasim Akram's response to allegations that his team had thrown the match was that these were 'blatant attempts to undermine our sterling performances in the World Cup and hamper our progress towards the final'.

Some days nothing goes right. The frustration is evident on the face of Pakistan fast bowler Waqar Younis as Bangladesh head towards a competitive total of 223 for nine.
(Getty Images/Touchline Photo)

ICC World Cup, 1999, 29th Match
Bangladesh v Pakistan, Group B
County Ground, Northampton
31 May 1999 (50-over match)

Result: Bangladesh won by 62 runs

Bangladesh innings
Shahriar Hossain lbw b Saqlain Mushtaq 39
Mehrab Hossain st Moin Khan b Saqlain Mushtaq 9
Akram Khan c Wasim Akram b Waqar Younis 47
*Aminul Islam b Shahid Afridi 15
Naimur Rahman b Waqar Younis 13
Minhajul Abedin c & b Saqlain Mushtaq 14
Khaled Mahmud st Moin Khan b Saqlain Mushtaq ...27
+Khaled Mashud not out 15
Mohammad Rafique c Shoaib Akhtar b Saqlain Mushta ..6
Niamur Rashid lbw b Wasim Akram 1
Shafiuddin Ahmed not out 2
Extras (lb 5, w 28, nb 7) 40
Total (9 wickets, 50 overs) 223

FoW: 1-69 (Mehrab Hossain), 2-70 (Shahriar Hossain), 3-120 (Aminul Islam), 4-148 (Akram Khan), 5-148 (Naimur Rahman), 6-187 (Minhajul Abedin), 7-195 (Khaled Mahmud), 8-208 (Mohammad Rafique), 9-212 (Niamur Rashid).

Bowling	O	M	R	W
Waqar Younis	9	1	36	2
Shoaib Akhtar	8	0	30	0
Wasim Akram	10	0	35	1
Azhar Mahmood	8	0	56	0
Saqlain Mushtaq	10	1	35	5
Shahid Afridi	5	0	26	1

Pakistan innings
Saeed Anwar run out (Khaled Mashud) 9
Shahid Afridi c Mehrab Hossain b Khaled Mahmud ..2
Ijaz Ahmed b Shafiuddin Ahmed 0
Inzamam-ul-Haq lbw b Khaled Mahmud 7
Salim Malik lbw b Khaled Mahmud 5
Azhar Mahmood run out (Khaled Mashud) 29
*Wasim Akram c Shahriar Hossain b Minhajul Abedin ..29
+Moin Khan c Mehrab Hossain b Naimur Rahman ...18
Saqlain Mushtaq run out (Khaled Mashud) 21
Waqar Younis b Mohammad Rafique 11
Shoaib Akhtar not out 1
Extras (b 1, lb 6, w 21, nb 1) 29
Total (all out, 44.3 overs) 161

FoW: 1-5 (Shahid Afridi), 2-7 (Ijaz Ahmed), 3-26 (Saeed Anwar), 4-29 (Inzamam-ul-Haq), 5-42 (Salim Malik), 6-97 (Azhar Mahmood), 7-102 (Wasim Akram), 8-124 (Moin Khan), 9-160 (Waqar Younis), 10-161 (Saqlain Mushtaq).

Bowling	O	M	R	W
Khaled Mahmud	10	2	31	3
Shafiuddin Ahmed	8	0	26	1
Niamur Rashid	5	1	20	0
Mohammad Rafique	8	0	28	1
Minhajul Abedin	7	2	29	1
Naimur Rahman	6.3	2	20	1

The fact remains, however, that all the ingredients for match fixing were present. It was the final pool match in Group B and the result was irrelevant: Bangladesh could not qualify and Pakistan had won all their previous matches, ensuring that they would top the log come what may. Present in the Pakistan side was Salim Malik, the man who had offered bribes to Shane Warne and Mark Waugh to bowl badly in a Test match.

Additionally, Akram chose to put the opposition in to bat and personally gave away 12 runs in no-balls and wides in an otherwise miserly display. In fact Pakistan conceded 40 extras in the relatively modest Bangladesh total of 223 for nine, of which seven were no-balls and 28 wides. Only Akram Khan, with 42, bettered the extras total with the bat.

When Pakistan batted there were three run-outs and several batsmen were caught off poorly judged strokes. Khaled Mahmud won the man of the match award for his three for 31, but on a good batting pitch no one else got more than a single wicket and not one of the six bowlers used went at more than four an over. Nevertheless, the result stands and it went some way towards convincing the ICC to hasten its decision to award Bangladesh Test match status.

It was the second victory for Bangladesh in the tournament, following a 22-run win against Scotland in Edinburgh. The team's fanatical supporters were somewhat better treated at Raeburn Place than in their first match against New Zealand in Chelmsford. In a shameful display of ignorance, the ground that is home to the English county Essex greeted its Muslim guests with bacon sandwiches.

Even the greatest bowlers have their off days. Wasim Akram bowled four no-balls and eight wides against Bangladesh.
(Getty Images/Touchline Photo)

The first of five wickets for Pakistan's ace off-spinner Saqlain Mushtaq at Wantage Road, Northampton. Bangladeshi openers Shahriar and Mehrab Hossain put on 69 for the first wicket, but Mehrab managed just 9 of those from 42 balls. In an attempt to raise the run rate Mehrab perished, jumping down the pitch and missing. Moin Khan removes the bails.
(Getty Images/Touchline Photo)

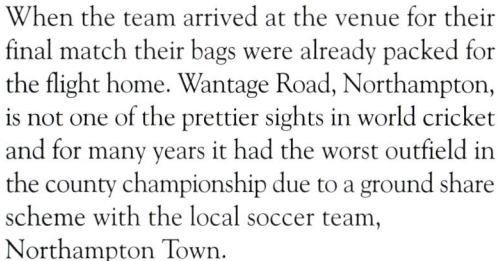

Facing page: Akram Khan's 42 was the highest score in the match between Bangladesh and Pakistan at the 1999 World Cup. Here he powerfully hits Azhar Mahmood back over his head.
(Getty Images/Touchline Photo)

When the team arrived at the venue for their final match their bags were already packed for the flight home. Wantage Road, Northampton, is not one of the prettier sights in world cricket and for many years it had the worst outfield in the county championship due to a ground share scheme with the local soccer team, Northampton Town.

But there was plenty of support for both sides and a party atmosphere prevailed for most of the day. Put in to bat, Mehrab and Shahriar Hossain gave Bangladesh an excellent start, scoring 69 runs off the first 15 overs and dealing somewhat casually with the threat of the fastest bowler at the tournament, Shoaib Akhtar. Shoaib shared the new ball with Waqar Younis, playing his only match of the tournament, and it was plain to see at that stage that there was little to fear from the seamers on a true pitch.

Akram brought his best spinner, Saqlain Mushtaq, into the attack as soon as the field restrictions were relaxed at the end of the 15th over and it was the off-spinner who kept the innings in check as he took five for 35 in a miserly spell. But the middle order hit out and ran hard and 223 was comfortably Bangladesh's best score of the tournament.

Only the ever-mounting extras column gave any clue to would-be conspiracy theorists at this stage, but when Pakistan batted it was a different story. Shahid Afridi miscued to point, Ijaz Ahmed dragged on to his stumps and Saeed Anwar unwisely relied on Inzamam-ul-Haq for a sharp single. Inzamam, the world's worst runner between the wickets, and Salim Malik were both lbw to Mahmud and Pakistan were 42 for five.

Bangladesh captain Aminul Islam is bowled by Shahid Afridi for 15. Afridi's quicker ball, a top spinner, has accounted for plenty of batsmen. The wicketkeeper is Moin Khan.
(Getty Images/Touchline Photo)

From there it was a question of survival. Akram and Azhar Mahmood put on 55 for the sixth wicket and there was a stand of 36 for the ninth, but the batting side was simply never in it. Bangladesh won with 5.4 overs to spare, prompting delirious celebrations among hundreds of supporters who raced on to the pitch before the third umpire could confirm the fall of the final wicket. Fortunately television showed that Saqlain Mushtaq had not made his ground, sparing stewards and police the task of clearing the pitch.

Bangladesh's captain, Aminul Islam, was the most delighted man of all and said that he hoped his country would proclaim a national holiday in honour of the team's extraordinary win. The allegations came soon enough, but this, to date, was Bangladesh's greatest cricketing moment.

The Pakistani section of the crowd at Wantage Road in Northampton seems content at the way their team is progressing against Bangladesh in the final first-round match of the 1999 World Cup. But the gentleman in the centre, known as 'Mr Cricket', has an intriguing look on his face. Does he suspect that the result is not going to go Pakistan's way?
(Getty Images/Touchline Photo)

Zimbabwe

A decade after gaining Test status it is something of an anachronism that Zimbabwe is still capable of producing a cricket team that, on its day, can beat all comers. During the run-up to the elections of 2002 the rule of law in the country had broken down to the extent that Dennis Streak, father of the national cricket captain Heath Streak, was kidnapped and threatened with his life for the heinous crime of owning a game farm. Yet, in the same month that Robert Mugabe was re-elected president of Zimbabwe, the country's cricketers toured India and produced a number of results that, given the circumstances, can only be described as extraordinary.

In 2002 there are probably not more than twenty players in Zimbabwe capable of playing cricket to international standard, yet on they go, touring the world, losing more games than they win, but producing on occasion performances that warm the hearts of those people (and cricket produces more than its fair share of them) who love an underdog.

They have been doing more or less the same thing for a decade now. The 1992 World Cup in Australia and New Zealand was Zimbabwe's final tournament as an associate member of the ICC. Later that year they were given full Test status and they played their first match against India in Harare between 18 and 22 October 1992. It turned out to be an eminently forgettable Test match, and most Zimbabweans would point to a game played seven months earlier as their team's finest moment of a momentous year.

The whole Zimbabwean team celebrates after beating England by nine runs in Albury.
(Getty Images/Touchline Photo)

England Defeated in Albury

This was the first time the two teams had ever met in a match, Zimbabwe having played all the other Test teams at least once before meeting England. After a desperately disappointing tournament Zimbabwe at last found the slow Albury pitch ideally suited their medium-fast seam attack, as well as giving slow turn to the spinners. England at this stage were, along with New Zealand, the most successful team in the World Cup. They had won five of their matches and lost only one (against New Zealand) and so were certain of their place in the semi-finals. Two World Cups later a similar situation in the match between Pakistan and Bangladesh raised the ugly spectre of match fixing, but these were, apparently, more innocent times.

Dave Houghton, Zimbabwe's finest player for whom Test status came ten years too late, played the best innings, dragging the team out of the depths of 30 for three, but even he never felt settled or able to master the conditions. He was eventually out trying to pull Gladstone Small, the ball coming off the splice and spooning to midwicket. After being put in Zimbabwe's eventual total of 134 was their lowest in twenty one-day internationals played by the team to that date and the senior players believed it was 40 or 50 shy of being defendable.

Eddo Brandes likes bowling against England. Here he clean bowls Robin Smith in Albury during the 1992 World Cup on his way to four for 21 from 10 overs.
(Getty Images/Touchline Photo)

Benson & Hedges World Cup, 1991/92
England v Zimbabwe
Lavington Sports Oval, Albury
18 March 1992 (50-overs match)

Result: Zimbabwe won by 9 runs

Zimbabwe innings
WR James *c* & *b* Illingworth 13
+A Flower *b* DeFreitas 7
AJ Pycroft *c* Gooch *b* Botham 3
KJ Arnott lbw *b* Botham 11
*DL Houghton *c* Fairbrother *b* Small 29
AC Waller *b* Tufnell 8
AH Shah *c* Lamb *b* Tufnell 3
IP Butchart *c* Fairbrother *b* Botham 24
EA Brandes *st* Stewart *b* Illingworth 14
AJ Traicos not out 0
MP Jarvis lbw *b* Illingworth 6
Extras (lb 8, w 8) 16
Total (all out, 46.1 overs) 134

FoW: 1-12 (Flower), 2-19 (Pycroft), 3-30 (James), 4-52 (Arnott), 5-65 (Waller), 6-77 (Omarshah), 7-96 (Houghton), 8-127 (Butchart), 9-127 (Brandes), 10-134 (Jarvis).

Bowling	O	M	R	W
DeFreitas	8	1	14	1
Small	9	1	20	1
Botham	10	2	23	3
Illingworth	9.1	0	33	3
Tufnell	10	2	36	2

England innings
*GA Gooch lbw *b* Brandes 0
IT Botham *c* Flower *b* Omarshah 18
AJ Lamb *c* James *b* Brandes 17
RA Smith *b* Brandes 2
GA Hick *b* Brandes 0
NH Fairbrother *c* Flower *b* Butchart 20
+AJ Stewart *c* Waller *b* Omarshah 29
PAJ DeFreitas *c* Flower *b* Butchart 4
RK Illingworth run out 11
GC Small *c* Pycroft *b* Jarvis 5
PCR Tufnell not out 0
Extras (b 4, lb 3, w 11, nb 1) 19
Total (all out, 49.1 overs) 125

FoW: 1-0 (Gooch), 2-32 (Lamb), 3-42 (Botham), 4-42 (Smith), 5-43 (Hick), 6-95 (Stewart), 7-101 (DeFreitas), 8-108 (Fairbrother), 9-124 (Illingworth), 10-125 (Small).

Bowling	O	M	R	W
Brandes	10	4	21	4
Jarvis	9.1	0	32	1
Shah	10	3	17	2
Traicos	10	4	16	0
Butchart	10	1	32	2

But Eddo Brandes began with a brilliant spell of outswing bowling, taking four wickets to break the back of the England innings. In an unbroken spell he conceded only 21 runs, of which 8 came in one over courtesy of two edges by Ian Botham. Graham Gooch was out to the first ball of the innings, lbw as he shuffled across his stumps and tried to work a low inswinging full toss away on the leg-side.

Botham and Allan Lamb then put on 32 together at which point Brandes bowled a bouncer and Lamb mistimed a pull to loop a catch to mid-on. The slow-medium Ali Shah came on first change and immediately had Botham well caught at the wicket by Andy Flower standing up to the stumps. Brandes then dismissed Robin Smith and his old schoolmate Graeme Hick in quick succession. Hick had played for his country of birth before signing for Worcestershire and qualified for England by residence. When he was out England were, astonishingly, 43 for five.

Even now the Zimbabweans did not entertain any real hopes of winning the match. Neil Fairbrother and Alec Stewart dug in, adding 52 together for the sixth wicket, but the partnership lasted more than 25 overs, at a rate of just two runs per over, something of a liability even with a target of only 135.

Shah and John Traicos, the slowest bowlers in the team, were mainly responsible, bowling their 20 overs for only 33 runs. Traicos bowled particularly well and proved throughout the tournament that, at the advanced age of forty-four and in a losing side, he was the finest off-spinner in world cricket. In the days when Zimbabwe was Rhodesia and playing as a provincial side in the Currie Cup, Traicos had played in South Africa's final Test before isolation, against Australia in 1969. Twenty-three years later he represented his country of birth in their first Test.

A special moment for Brandes as he bowls Graeme Hick for a duck, reducing England to 43 for five. Brandes went to school with Hick in Zimbabwe and Hick had played for his country of birth before signing for Worcestershire and qualifying for England by residence.
(Getty Images/Touchline Photo)

But it was Shah who eventually made the breakthrough, dismissing Stewart, superbly caught by Andy Waller diving low in the covers as he checked a drive. Iain Butchart had both Phil DeFreitas and Fairbrother caught at the wicket in quick succession, then Richard Illingworth and Gladstone Small ground out 16 runs together, but with 23 needed from the last four overs the pressure was mounting. Then they had a mix-up over a run, both being stranded in the middle of the pitch. Kevin Arnott, who fielded the ball brilliantly at midwicket threw down the stumps at the bowler's end.

The last pair needed to score 10 runs off the last over to win and Houghton entrusted it to the steady Malcolm Jarvis, who had been bowling a lot of slower balls getting spin and cut off the pitch. Houghton told him to bowl his slower delivery first ball and he obliged; so did Small, who flicked the ball off his toes and lobbed a simple catch to midwicket to give Zimbabwe a remarkable victory.

I watched the game on television at home in England and later in the day the power of sport was brought home to me. I was watching Top of the Pops, the BBC's most venerable popular music show, when on came a New Zealand band, Crowded House, singing their current hit, 'Weather With You'. In the middle of the instrumental break, lead singer Neil Finn looked straight into the camera and said, 'Yo, Zimbabwe!' a reference that was lost on ninety-nine per cent of his audience, but still makes me chuckle all these years later.

At the 1992 World Cup John Traicos proved that, at the advanced age of forty-four and in a losing side, he was the finest off-spinner in world cricket. In the days when Zimbabwe was Rhodesia and playing as a provincial side in the Currie Cup, Traicos had played in South Africa's final Test before isolation, against Australia in 1969. Twenty-three years later he represented his country of birth in their first Test. Umpire Venkat, a Test off-spinner himself and a former captain of India, looks on approvingly.
(Getty Images/Touchline Photo)

Chicken George Stuffs England

Chicken George Stuffs England. Eddo Brandes celebrates the wicket of Nick Knight, caught down the leg-side by wicketkeeper Andy Flower. The smile on Brandes' face is tempered by the fact that he knew it was a lucky dismissal, but the next two were anything but.
(Getty Images/Touchline Photo)

The meat in the sandwich. John Crawley was the second wicket in Eddo Brandes' hat-trick at Harare Sports Club, plumb lbw to the first ball of his third over.
(Getty Images/Touchline Photo)

Five years after Zimbabwe had earned full Test status England toured there, playing two Tests and three ODIs. It was an acrimonious tour in many ways, for in the second Test in Bulawayo Zimbabwe bowled wide down the leg-side in the final hour to avoid defeat, a tactic that temporarily loosened the mind of the England coach, David Lloyd.

In the post-match press conference I suggested to the normally affable Lloyd that England had had the worst of most of the first four days and that any side would have adopted negative bowling tactics in the circumstances. But Lloyd would have none of it and attempted to rewrite history by uttering the now infamous phrase, 'We flippin' murdered them.' When I sought out the Zimbabwe captain Alistair Campbell for his thoughts on the game and told him what Lloyd had said, he questioned the England coach's sanity.

The ODI series therefore began under a cloud, but as if to prove to Lloyd that there was more than one team on the field, Zimbabwe cruised to a 3-0 series victory and saved the best moment till last.

England, having put Zimbabwe in to bat and been flogged around for 249, collapsed to 118 all out in just 30 overs as the top order was decimated by an Eddo Brandes hat-trick, only the tenth in one-day internationals (at the time) and – a little more surprisingly – the first against England. Brandes was a chicken farmer from just outside Harare who had been persuaded out of semi-retirement to play against England. He was known to his team mates as 'Chicken George' and this was the day that the chicken stuffed England.

Most one-day hat-tricks involve lower-order batsmen slogging, but this one cleaned up the cream of England's batting. Brandes's first victim, Nick Knight, thin-edged a leg-side catch to the wicketkeeper, having made three. Knight was out to the final ball of Brandes' second over. The first ball of his third found John Crawley playing across a straight delivery to be lbw for a duck, so far so unmemorable.

Next ball Nasser Hussain was brilliantly caught by Andy Flower off a perfect outswinger and the hat-trick was complete.
(Getty Images/Touchline Photo)

But the hat-trick ball was undeniably special. The perfect length drew Nasser Hussain forward, the ball swung late to take the outside edge, and wicketkeeper Andy Flower took a stunning full-length catch low down in front of first slip. The crowd (and some of the press) at the Harare Sports Club went wild. England were 13 for three. Who was murdering whom? A banner in the crowd summed matters up. It said, 'Never mind the white rhino, save the Poms'.

Brandes continued to bowl superbly, picking up Alec Stewart with another late outswinger and getting Michael Atherton (who had virtually resumed his opener's spot despite coming in at number five) with one that lifted and left him. From 54 for five there was no way back for England, and all that remained was to try to pass their previous lowest one-day score, 93 in the 1975 World Cup semi-final against Australia at Headingley. At 77 for eight they were odds against, but some desperate slogging finally lifted them past three figures before the last two wickets went down off consecutive balls. No fewer than five batsmen were out for a duck.

It was the end of the series and, knowing that friends back in South Africa would be wanting souvenirs, I bought half a dozen Zimbabwe caps at the tented village. Bumping into Campbell later that night I pressed a cap on him, which he duly signed and then added a caustic comment: 'We flippin' murdered them', he wrote. Still in a party mood I packed my things the following day and flew to Victoria Falls where I proposed to the lovely lady who is now my wife.

Zimbabwe v England, 1996/97
Harare Sports Club
3 January 1997 (50-overs match)

Result: Zimbabwe won by 131 runs
Zimbabwe wins the 3-ODI series 3-0

Zimbabwe innings
GW Flower c Mullally b White 62
AC Waller run out (Atherton) 19
*ADR Campbell not out 80
+A Flower c Stewart b Irani 35
CN Evans c Stewart b Gough 1
GJ Whittall b Croft 1
DL Houghton c Stewart b Mullally 19
PA Strang run out (White) 13
Extras (b 4, lb 5, w 8, nb 2) 19
Total (7 wickets, 50 overs) 249

DNB: HH Streak, EA Brandes, JA Rennie.

FoW: 1-58 (Waller), 2-131 (GW Flower), 3-181 (A Flower), 4-183 (Evans), 5-190 (Whittall), 6-220 (Houghton), 7-249 (Strang).

Bowling	O	M	R	W
Mullally	10	3	39	1
Gough	10	1	42	1
Silverwood	5	0	27	0
White	7	0	39	1
Irani	10	0	39	1
Croft	8	0	54	1

England innings
NV Knight c A Flower b Brandes 3
+AJ Stewart c A Flower b Brandes 29
JP Crawley lbw b Brandes 0
N Hussain c A Flower b Brandes 0
*MA Atherton c A Flower b Brandes 18
RC Irani c Whittall b Streak 0
C White c A Flower b Streak 0
RDB Croft not out 30
D Gough c Streak b Strang 7
AD Mullally b Whittall 20
CEW Silverwood c Evans b Whittall 0
Extras (w 8, nb 3) 11
Total (all out, 30 overs) 118

FoW: 1-9 (Knight), 2-13 (Crawley), 3-13 (Hussain), 4-45 (Stewart), 5-54 (Atherton), 6-55 (Irani), 7-63 (White), 8-77 (Gough), 9-118 (Mullally), 10-118 (Silverwood).

Bowling	O	M	R	W
Brandes	10	0	28	5
Rennie	3	0	11	0
Streak	10	0	50	2
Strang	5	0	18	1
Whittall	2	0	11	2

Marillier's Magic

While Zimbabweans were preparing to go to the polls back home in Africa, the national cricket team was in India. The Test series was lost despite some magnificent batting from Andy Flower, but the tourists got off to the perfect start in the five-match ODI series thanks to one of the most amazing innings ever played by anybody, anywhere.

Batting first, India put up a commanding total of 274 for 6, with half-centuries of rare pedigree from Sourav Ganguly (57) and VVS Laxman (75). But a miserly spell of slow left-arm from Grant Flower in mid-innings put the brakes on and when Ajay Ratra was run out it was 211 for six with only 6.2 overs remaining in the innings.

Those final overs were to yield 63 precious runs, however, as Ajit Agarkar, once known as 'The Bombay Duck' for his run of noughts in Test cricket, blitzed 40 not out off just 19 balls with six fours and a six. Among the men who suffered was Doug Marillier. The medium pacer's 10 overs went for 53 runs, but some three hours later he had his revenge, and how!

Even on a blameless Faridabad pitch Zimbabwe knew they needed a good start. Instead they were 21 for two when Andy Flower joined Alistair Campbell. As long as those two classy left-handers were together there was a chance. Flower, in particular, was in the form of his life and had been the best batsman in world cricket in 2001. He particularly enjoyed Indian conditions and made a misery of the lives of their spin bowlers with the reverse sweep, a shot he perfected to the point where it could scarcely be categorised as mildly irresponsible, let alone risky.

The pair added 111 in 22 overs and Flower was desperately unlucky to drag a wide ball from Anil Kumble on to his stumps with the score on 132. Flower's 71 came off 72 balls with two sixes and eight fours. Zimbabwe captain Stuart Carlisle then gave Campbell good support and the fourth-wicket pair put on 54 in 10 overs, but Ganguly's decision to bring back his best bowler, left-arm seamer Zaheer Khan, sent the innings into a spin. Carlisle was caught behind by Ajay Ratra off Khan for 23 and Campbell fell lbw to the first ball of Khan's next over for 84. From 186 for three Zimbabwe had collapsed to 210 for eight, at which point, with 65 needed from 5.4 overs, Douglas Anthony Marillier walked to the crease.

Marillier was twenty-three years old and in the team for his seam bowling. That he was playing cricket at all was something of a miracle; he had been involved in a terrible car crash some years earlier, nearly lost his life and was told at one stage that he would never walk again. As can happen when people have stared death in the face, Marillier's character developed a devil-may-care side and there were even those prepared to suggest that he was mad!

Andy Flower might be the best batsman in the world against spin bowling, but the pacemen also know not to bowl short at him.
(Getty Images/Touchline Photo)

Left: *Andy Flower may not be the best wicketkeeper in the world, but he catches most of the nicks that come his way. Then there's his batting, of course.*
(Getty Images/Touchline Photo)

Andy Flower where he likes to be, down on one knee dominating the spinners.
(Getty Images/Touchline Photo)

Marillier joined teenage wicketkeeper Taitenda Taibu at the wicket and said afterwards: 'There was no thought process. When I came in we needed 65 and the only way was to hit a few boundaries.' Marillier hit his first ball for a single and when he got the strike back for the last ball of the over he ran down the pitch, didn't quite get there and, aiming for extra cover, sliced the ball down to third man for four.

At this early stage of the innings third man was Marillier's main scoring area. He hit two fours down there in Anil Kumble's next over, but with only four left in the innings the rate required was now 12. Cricketers talk of the importance of 'big overs' in a run chase, meaning an over towards the end of an innings that goes for 10 or more runs, brings the required rate down and eases some of the pressure on the batting side. Zimbabwe's 'big over' was the 47th of the innings and was bowled by Zaheer Khan. At its beginning, Khan's figures were 8-2-15-4, at its end 9-2-35-4.

The first ball went down to third man for two, the second through cover for four. Now Marillier's innings entered its fascinating second stage when, with the off-side field loaded, he decided to exploit the gaps behind square on the leg-side. The third ball of Khan's over (a no ball) was a good length and on off stump. Marillier walked across his stumps and flicked it over the keeper's head for two. He missed the next, but a full toss on leg stump was smashed for six over midwicket next ball and that was followed by another saunter across to the off-side to flick the ball over fine leg's head for four.

Having stolen the strike with a single off the last ball, Marillier hit a boundary through the covers off the first ball of Sanjay Bangar's next over, then took a single. The pendulum then swung back India's way. The fourth ball of the over was so wide that Taibu couldn't reach it, but was given out anyway, allegedly caught behind for eight. He and Marillier had added 42 in 21 balls.

Last man Gary Brent could make nothing of the last two balls of the over and with Khan to bowl the 49th over 23 runs were required and the last pair together. Marillier missed the first, scampered a leg-bye off the second (a no-ball) and got the strike back for the fifth when Brent ran a leg-bye off the fourth delivery. Three runs of the 23 required had been gathered and there were now only eight balls left in the innings.

But, crucially, Khan overstepped again, Marillier whipped his slower ball over the keeper's head for four, did the same to the next and then pushed one wide of point to keep the strike.

With 10 needed off the last over Ganguly brought on the one bowler that any captain of the previous decade would have been pleased to have in his side in the circumstances, Anil Kumble. The bespectacled leg-spinner had forged a reputation as one of the hardest bowlers to hit in world cricket, but Marillier as it turned out was no respecter of reputations. Giving himself room to Kumble's first ball he thrashed it through the covers for four to reach his 50 off 21 balls with nine fours and a six!

Before his remarkable half century against India this was the kind of batting most people associated with Doug Marillier, bowled neck and crop by England's James Kirtley.
(Getty Images/Touchline Photo)

He took one off the next, exposing Brent to the strike with five needed off four balls. Many would have panicked in the situation, but Brent calmly pushed the ball down to long-off for a single. Marillier back on strike, four to win, three balls left. Struck on the pads by Kumble's next ball, Marillier knew that all his previous deeds would count for nothing if he could not score the winning runs and now there were only two balls left.

Ganguly spent an age discussing where to put his fielders with Kumble and Sachin Tendulkar, meanwhile Marillier met with Brent and suggested that, rather than risk a run-out, he would try and hit a boundary. Eventually Kumble bowled, but dropped short: Marillier rocked on to the back foot and, attempting to pull the ball through midwicket, instead top-edged it down to third man for the winning boundary. When the dust settled it transpired that Kumble had overstepped and Marillier's hit was worth five to the team, not four.

He finished 56 not out from 24 balls, having scored all but nine of the 65 required when he came to the crease in an apparently hopeless situation. After the game he was the coolest man on the ground, saying, 'In the circumstances the way I played was irrelevant. (Zimbabwe coach) Geoff Marsh would crucify me if I batted like that in the nets. I only took up bowling late in my career, I started as a batsman, but the way I played today maybe they'll push me up to number nine!'

It is frequently said that the safest place to hit any bowler is back over his head, but in this innings Marillier proved otherwise. Some years earlier Javed Miandad perfected the leg-glance to a ball pitching outside off stump, but Marillier used the full face of the bat to a club a ball that had already passed his body, over the wicketkeeper's head. There's a good reason why this shot is not in any coaching manual: it's damn near impossible.

If Marillier had got out the first time he played it in this innings the match would have passed by unnoticed, but he didn't and by the end he was middling the ball with his 'impossible' shot. The bush telegraph is alive and well in cricket and a number of people who watched the television images will go into the nets and try to 'do a Marillier'. If a few of them find a way to play it without too great a risk, the Marillier shot may become the reverse sweep of the next decade and bowlers will have yet another reason to bemoan the fact that one-day cricket is unfairly loaded towards batsmen.

India v Zimbabwe
Nahar Singh Stadium, Faridabad
7 March 2002 (50-over match)

Result: Zimbabwe won by 1 wicket

India innings
D Mongia c Taibu b Streak 25
*SC Ganguly st Taibu b Marillier 57
VVS Laxman run out (Ebrahim/GW Flower) 75
R Dravid lbw b GW Flower 23
M Kaif not out 39
SB Bangar c Friend b Streak 0
+A Ratra run out (A Flower/Marillier) 6
AB Agarkar not out 40
Extras (lb 1, w 6, nb 2) 9
Total (6 wickets, 50 overs) 274

DNB: A Kumble, Harbhajan Singh, Z Khan.

FoW: 1-46 (Mongia), 2-123 (Ganguly), 3-171 (Dravid), 4-193 (Laxman), 5-193 (Bangar), 6-211 (Ratra).

Bowling	O	M	R	W
Streak	10	0	53	2
Friend	10	0	68	0
Brent	10	0	68	0
Marillier	10	0	53	1
GW Flower	10	0	31	1

Zimbabwe innings
ADR Campbell lbw b Khan 84
CB Wishart b Khan 1
TJ Friend b Khan 7
A Flower b Kumble 71
*SV Carlisle c Ratra b Khan 23
DD Ebrahim c Ganguly b Bangar 10
GW Flower c & b Harbhajan Singh 2
HH Streak c Ganguly b Harbhajan Singh 1
+T Taibu c Ratra b Bangar 8
DA Marillier not out 56
GB Brent not out 1
Extras (lb 4, w 2, nb 6) 12
Total (9 wickets, 49.4 overs) 276

FoW: 1-5 (Wishart), 2-21 (Friend), 3-132 (A Flower), 4-186 (Carlisle), 5-193 (Campbell), 6-198 (GW Flower), 7-200 (Streak), 8-210 (Ebrahim), 9-252 (Taibu).

Bowling	O	M	R	W
Khan	10	2	47	4
Agarkar	8	0	45	0
Bangar	9	0	42	2
Harbhajan Singh	10	1	48	2
Kumble	9.4	0	70	1
Ganguly	3	0	20	0

Epilogue

The question that the ICC will have to answer before too long is whether they are correct in assuming that Test cricket is the most important form of the game. If it is, why are there so many empty seats at Test matches and so few at ODIs? One-day cricket was conceived as a method of bringing the public back to the game: it succeeded beyond the wildest dreams. Why, then, do we still have to make excuses for one-day cricket? It's fun, but it's not real cricket. People love it, but that's because they don't understand Test cricket. Instead of trotting out the same old conservative clichés, why not adopt a French motto: *Vive la difference.*

The first class game is legendary for its lack of excess, hazarding a larger set of stumps in the 1930s, a change in the no-ball law in the 1960s, and settling for cosmetic exercises in most other cases. The civil service law prevails: many things must be done, but nothing must be done for the first time. The reason that one-day cricket is so successful is because it is not afraid to change. The Gillette Cup began as a 65 overs a side monster, but forty years later the English counties are about to embark on a new competition of just 20 overs a side. In evolutionary terms that's like mankind deciding within four generations to grow an extra leg!

In the 1970s it was feared that one-day cricket would ruin technique. Instead, another Darwinian law applied: survival of the fittest. It is no longer enough to have the kind of impregnable defence that marked out Geoffrey Boycott. You won't get a first class contract if you can't score at close to a run a ball and, it goes without saying, you can't score at a run a ball if you're sat in the pavilion bemoaning an unplayable one that removed your middle stump. One-day cricket has galvanised Test cricket with its dynamism and, more than that, it has lifted the standard of batting, bowling and, particularly, fielding.

It has also had positive spin-offs for the attempted globalisation of the game. There is a rule in boxing that states, 'A good big 'un will always beat a good little 'un.' The evidence of this book suggests that it is a dictum that is not applicable to ODIs. To be sure, a series of five or seven matches between the same two teams will inevitably reveal where the balance of power lies, but one-off games, especially at neutral venues, frequently produce unusual results.

The ICC is not a body given to revolutionary thinking, but one of the best decisions it ever made was to introduce ODI status for Kenya and Bangladesh. The latter has already gone on to full Test status and it is a question of when, not if, for Kenya from here on. The path has been eased by the greater frequency of international contact available for countries in the higher echelons. So, while it took New Zealand decades to produce a competitive Test team, Sri Lanka were a force to be reckoned with less than ten years after receiving Test status and, while their results are dismal at the moment, there is little doubt that Bangladesh will produce a formidable side sooner rather than later.

When that happens we will look back at their development as a one-day side and note that all they really needed was experience. And, as the poet said, experience is not bought for the price of a song, nor wisdom for a dance in the street. But, and here's the key, victory in the World Cup would have the effect of setting a whole nation dancing in the street. Only one-day cricket can do that and it's high time we stopped making excuses for it so that we can celebrate it for what it is: the very lifeblood of the game.